THE T-SHAPED LAWYER GUIDEBOOK

A Framework for Your Professional Development

peter.connor@alternativelylegal.com

www.linkedin.com/in/petercon

Self-published by Peter Connor.

First printing and publication 2024.

ISBN: 978-0-6486002-9-9 for eBook
ISBN: 978-0-6486002-6-8 for paperback

TABLE OF CONTENTS

FOREWORD

INTRODUCTION

CHAPTER 1

ALIGNING THE PERSONAL WITH THE PROFESSIONAL

A. Your wellbeing and wellness at work

B. Understanding yourself – all the things that make you unique.

C. How to align 'your personal' with 'your professional'

CHAPTER 2

OVERVIEW OF THE T-SHAPED LAWYER FRAMEWORK™

A. Why the need for the Framework.

B. Transformative Learning – effective learning for adults.

C. What is included in the Framework and why.

D. Answering common questions about The Framework

CHAPTER 3

T-SHAPED LAWYER SKILLS

A. Business Partnering and Business Leadership – The Super Skills

B. Risk Assessment not just Legal Risk Assessment

C. Technology not just Legal Technology

D. Process Improvement not just Legal Process Improvement

E. Project Management not just Legal Project Management

F. Design Thinking not just Legal Design

CHAPTER 4

T-SHAPED LAWYER COMPETENCIES

A. Leadership

B. Change Management

C. Innovation

D. Teamwork and Collaboration

E. Networking

F. Communication

G. Problem Solving

H. Critical Thinking

I. Emotional Intelligence

CHAPTER 5

T-SHAPED LAWYER QUALITIES

A. Curiosity

B. Creativity

C. Empathy

D. Adaptability

E. Resilience

F. Integrity

CHAPTER 6

T-SHAPED LAWYER KNOWLEDGE

A. Business

B. Client

C. Technology

D. Legal Industry

CHAPTER 7

T-SHAPED LAWYER MINDSETS

A. The basics of mindsets

B. The Businessperson Mindset™

C. The Growth Mindset®

D. The Innovators Mindset®

CHAPTER 8

HOW TO USE THE T-SHAPED LAWYER FRAMEWORK

A. As individual lawyers

B. As individuals who are not lawyers

C. As leaders/managers of legal departments and firms

CONCLUSION

APPENDIX: GLOSSARY FOR CHANGE IN THE CORPORATE LEGAL INDUSTRY

ABOUT THE AUTHOR

FOREWORD

Rajah Tann Asia (RTA) is a leading law firm with almost one thousand lawyers in offices in 10 countries throughout Asia.

The RTA management, with their commitment to the growth and wellbeing of our professionals, developed the vision that our lawyers should become multi-skilled legal and business professionals, with the relevant organisational support.

To achieve this vision, the RTA Academy was set up in 2019 to curate diverse, interactive, accessible in-person and online professional development programs for our legal and business communities.

To ensure structured development of core non-legal skills and competencies that are aligned with our goals, we reached out to Peter Connor, whose T-Shaped Lawyer programs and work with a wide variety of law firm and in-house clients in Asia and other parts of the world, served this goal purposefully and directly.

His T-Shaped Lawyer vision, the subject of his first book, is a good reflection of our vision for the multi-skilled legal and business professional, and we have used his T-Shaped Lawyer Framework™ to curate and structure content for our communities.

From 2020, I have had the pleasure of working closely with Peter to refine his framework for our specific purposes, and to build out a comprehensive program for our network. The programs we have built include level definitions, assessment tools and practices, and a range of different content delivered in diverse ways to ensure easy access for our regional legal and business professionals. The feedback has been extremely positive.

Peter's second book, *The T-Shaped Lawyer Framework*, provides an insightful overview of that comprehensive framework, and I believe it is imperative that every legal or business professional, regardless of whether they work in a corporate law firm or in-house legal department, take the time to read it. It is, as Peter states, an essential travel guide to one's learning and career journey especially if you aspire to be a T-Shaped Lawyer.

It should also provide every firm and in-house department with insights about how to adopt a structured approach to professional development for your teams, that goes beyond an ad hoc selection of non-legal skills and competency training.

When you reflect on this book, together with Peter's first book, *The T-Shaped Lawyer: A New Vision for You and Your Work*, it will become apparent that the ideas extend beyond professional development. Peter has highlighted these game changing ideas to our regional leadership team, and this has enhanced their thinking around strategy, innovation, transformation, culture, offerings, and ways of working.

There is no substitute for having Peter guide you along this new path, but these books are the next best thing.

Santhi Latha

Dean

Rajah & Tann Asia Academy

INTRODUCTION

If you are reading this book then you are almost certainly not one of the many lawyers who view professional development as optional, a 'nice to have,' or as a 'tick-the-box' exercise to meet your continuing professional development requirements for your practising certificate.

Rather, you probably:

- understand that you need to 'own' your career and drive your training and development. Your manager and others can help. However, it is a mistake to just do your work well and leave it up to them to ensure that you gain the necessary work experiences and training.
- have limited time and money to invest in learning, training and professional development and want to maximise the return on that investment.
- realise that to be successful and fulfilled it is no longer sufficient to understand the law and have great legal skills. However, you probably do not have a clear idea about what other capabilities you should develop and how to use them. This uncertainty is probably compounded by the vast variety of suggestions from others about what new skills you need.

This book is intended to address that problem by clarifying what new capabilities you need, explaining these to at least a basic level, and guiding you on how to use them to do not only legal work but also non-legal work in your role as a lawyer.

Forming a view about the work that you plan to do now and in the future is a critical first step before attempting to address this problem. If you do not do that, even if you understand the need to develop non-legal skills, you will:

- find it difficult, if not impossible, to decide which skills you should focus on because there is no reference point to help you make that decision.
- assume that the idea is to use these skills to do legal work. However, it should come as no surprise that non-legal skills are almost exclusively to help you do non-legal work.
- think that it is all about skills. It is about much more than that as I will explain in this book.

That is why I chose to cover this topic of professional development in a second book, after publishing my first book, *The T-Shaped Lawyer: A New Vision for You and Your Work*[1]. Although this second book stands on its own, I strongly encourage you to read the first book before reading this book.

In my first book I proposed a clear picture for you to consider in the form of a new direction and new work for corporate lawyers working in legal departments and law firms. Here are just a few of the key points from the first book to help set the scene for this second book. It:

- provided an overview of the changes happening in the world that are relevant to you as a corporate lawyer and your work. These changes provide context for you to consider what changes you should make for yourself and your work for the present and for the future.
- made the case for why you should transform yourself and your work to become a different lawyer; not just improve to be a better lawyer. The imperative for change is now even stronger with the rapid emergence of generative artificial intelligence that is, and will continue to, encroach on traditional legal work adding greater urgency to the need to find new work of the type proposed in that book.
- highlighted that, while each of you may have unique reasons to change, **the paramount change objective for all corporate lawyers should be to change your work so that you can add more value, especially for your clients.**
- explained that the key to addressing these reasons for change, and especially to be able to add more value for your clients, is to **transform to become a businessperson, not just a lawyer, and to provide business advice and input, not just legal advice, and do business work, not just legal work for the benefit of the business, not just the legal department or firm.**
- emphasised the simple equation: **Law + Business = 2x Value**
- proposed a new vision, **The T-Shaped Lawyer**, a version of the Legal Expert Business Generalist, that best embodies this specific transformation. See graphic below.

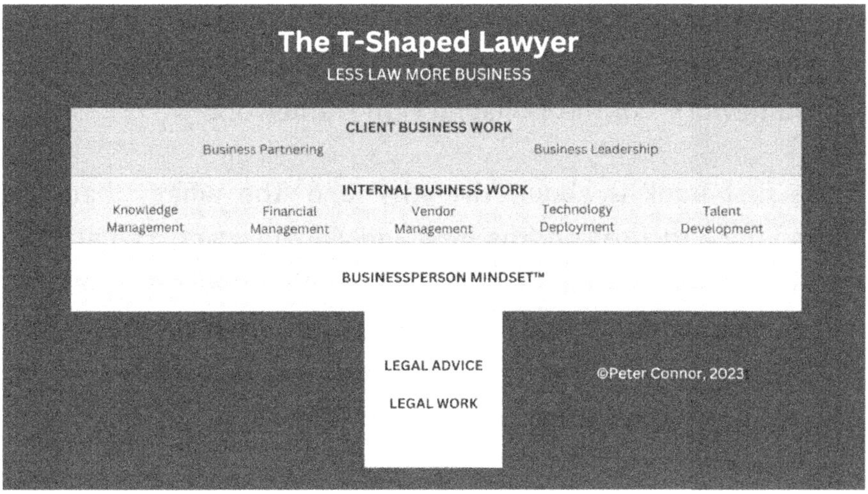

- fleshed out this vision by outlining what it means to be a businessperson and what it means to provide business advice and input and to do business work.
- explained that a lot of work you already do is NOT legal work and therefore, for corporate lawyers, it is business work.
- highlighted the crucial distinction between **internal business work** and **client business work** which will represent a central theme throughout this second book because it fundamentally changes the perspective on learning, training, and professional development.
- suggested that the best way to achieve this vision as individuals is to make the **Less Law More Business** pivot and to use the T-Shaped Lawyer Framework™ to change your capabilities to do this new work.
- pointed out that if this new vision resonates with leaders of legal departments and firms, they can not only support you

transforming in this way, but they can also redesign the legal department or firm along the lines of the T-Shaped Team Framework™ or the T-Shaped Firm Framework™.

If the first book is about **'the why'** and **'the what',** then this second book focuses on **'the how'** individual lawyers can achieve the new vision through a range of specific **mindsets, qualities, knowledge, competencies, and skills.** It explains the critical differences between these five dimensions and identifies various relevant component areas for each dimension.

The aim of this book is not to make you an expert in any one area. Rather the book will help you to understand each component, why it is important and how to develop it and use it in your work. That equates to a base level of competence. Individuals can then build on this base level by undertaking additional learning and on-the-job practice as explained in the book.

Leaders, and learning, human resource and training and development professionals, in legal departments and firms can also use this Framework to build out learning, training and professional development programs for their lawyers and other staff. Santhi Latha mentioned in the foreword to this book that Rajah Tann Asia ('RTA') has done exactly that. The primary benefit of using the Framework is to help lawyers become T-Shaped Lawyers or, as RTA calls it, ***'multi-skilled legal and business professionals'***. That vision provides the ***'new frame of reference'*** that Transformative Learning Theory tells us is so crucial for any learning to be meaningful and effective for adults.

As Santhi mentions, if that new vision resonates with a firm or legal department then what typically starts out as a focus on professional development and training then naturally leads to a reconsideration of everything else in the firm or legal department. As shown in the T-Shaped Team Framework™ and the T-Shaped Firm Framework™, it can impact culture, strategies, goals, metrics, resources, third party collaborators, and services and products offered. It reframes the way you currently look at everything and, as a result, can be game changing!

That said, the T-Shaped Lawyer Framework can also be used by individuals, legal departments, and firms with more conservative ambitions who do not aspire to that new vision. If you fall into this category, then at least the Framework offers a strategic structured approach to professional development that is much better than a random selection of non-legal skills.

The T-Shaped Lawyer Framework is not a set of random or arbitrary topics that I have read about. Rather, these are specific capabilities that helped me to become a T-Shaped Lawyer working for more than 25 years in-house and in a law firm in various countries all over the world. I was certainly not conscious of all these component areas when I was working as a lawyer. In fact, in the absence of such a framework, I opportunistically stumbled upon many of these components.

It is only since 2014, when I stopped working as a lawyer and started helping lawyers to work in new ways, that I have identified, defined, and refined these components into the T-Shaped Lawyer Framework. Since then, the Framework has been tested in my workshops with thousands of lawyers all over the world. I have also incorporated research and other expert opinions to substantiate or reinforce my own ideas and theories.

I am extremely grateful to Rajah Tann Asia and especially to Santhi and the RTA Academy. Over the last few years, they have played a critical part in helping to refine the Framework and deciding how best to use the Framework as the basis for a professional development program at a firm or legal department.

All references in this book, and the T-Shaped Lawyer Framework, to lawyers are specifically to corporate lawyers. By that I mean in-house lawyers or those who work for a law firm or other organisation that provides legal services to corporations.

That said, the Framework will also be of great interest to other lawyers such as government lawyers and to law students and academics. The first book and this second book will provide students and academics with a unique insight into what being a corporate lawyer is like in the 'real-world'. That should help students to decide whether a role as a lawyer, or as one of the growing other professional roles in the corporate legal industry, is for them. It should also help guide their choice of subjects to study and experiences to gain before starting full time work.

The first book, and the Framework in this second book, will also be of particular interest to the increasing number of professionals who are in roles in the corporate legal industry other than as a lawyer. It would have been too difficult to expand the scope of the books to cover these roles in more detail. However, the books should help to clarify where these professionals fit in and can add most value. Also, the Framework can quite easily be adapted to guide the professional development of these professionals.

The first book shows you that there is a new, and different, direction you can follow in your career that will take you to new and varied places along your journey to become a T-Shaped Lawyer. **If the first book is the map showing you the new direction, then this second book is a Lonely Planet-type travel companion guide to help you on your journey on that new path.**

Although I do act as a guide for individual lawyers, legal departments, and firms on this journey, I have written both books with the aim of providing individuals with the guidance to make this journey on your own.

I wish you well on your journey and hope that the books help to make sense of all the complexity and 'noise' in the corporate legal industry and provide you with the inspiration and guidance to thrive and find professional fulfilment and success.

CHAPTER 1

ALIGNING THE PERSONAL WITH THE PROFESSIONAL

The primary outcomes[2] that almost everyone working in a legal department or firm is seeking are professional success, personal growth, and fulfilment[3]. I refer to that as **'thriving' at work** and what that looks like varies greatly for every individual.

Despite what others may say, there is no 'magic bullet' that is going to guarantee you professional success and fulfilment. This book does not offer a magic bullet. Rather it offers a structured and holistic approach to enhance your prospects of thriving at work both now and in the future.

To thrive at work, it is essential to consider both personal and professional factors as depicted in the graphic below. Addressing just one of these two dimensions, as some do, is almost certain to fail.

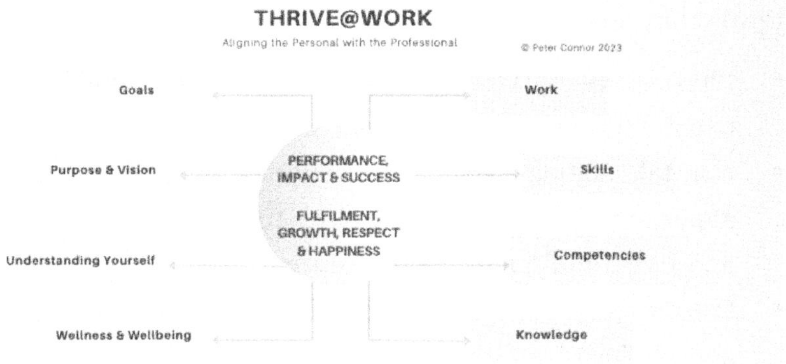

This book is primarily about the professional dimension - a topic that, especially compared with the personal dimension, is rarely covered in depth for corporate lawyers. That said, you will see that the Framework includes some very specific personal aspects. Also, **in this chapter I will briefly explain how you, and your managers and coaches, can incorporate some key personal factors, and combine them with the professional dimension, to help you thrive at work.**

Any discussion about professional development should start with analysing the personal dimension and that is what we will now briefly do.

A. <u>Your wellbeing and wellness at work</u>

Wellness and wellbeing are the foundations for thriving at work. In recent times there two increasingly important areas of concern for lawyers[4] and others. Some argue that lawyers face unique issues emanating from the way you are taught to think in law school[5] on top of the pressures of the workplace.

There are various definitions for these concepts but in broad terms they include the following inter-related states of being:

- **Physical**. Being able to undertake most activities within your capabilities without significant suffering.
- **Mental.** Being able to understand and process your experiences including the ability to reason through decisions and to maintain a focused attention span.
- **Emotional.** Being aware of and be able to manage your moods and feelings.
- **Financial.** Being able to provide at least a basic level of financial security and being in control of your finances.
- **Social.** Being able to create and maintain healthy reciprocal relationships, and have meaningful authentic interactions, with others.
- **Community.** Being, and feeling as if you are, a part of relevant real-world or virtual communities.

The impact of work

The workplace can impact your wellness and wellbeing positively or negatively including any or all the following ways:

- **Engagement.** There are many situations that can lead to you 'checking out' or not being engaged at work. A lack of meaning or purpose to your work can be one primary cause of lack of engagement. By contrast, when you find the work interesting and challenging, engagement and dedication typically follow naturally.
- **Health and safety**. There are many ways that work can give rise to health and safety issues for lawyers. Usually, physical safety is not an issue for lawyers although ergonomics and

office design factors should be considered. However, the relentless demands of the work typically done by most corporate lawyers can give rise to stress and mental health concerns. **In fact, you could argue that the traditional business model of law firms, and the default design of legal departments, necessarily results in an unhealthy situation where lawyers are constantly struggling to meet excessive work expectations. This is one reason why I encourage legal leaders to re-imagine and re-design this work as suggested in my first book and in my T-Shaped Team Framework™ and T-Shaped Firm Framework™.**

- **Psychological and emotional safety**. There are a variety of ways in which this very specific area of safety can contribute to, or detract from, your wellbeing and wellness. At one extreme would be psychosocial issues such as discrimination, workplace violence or sexual or other types of harassment. Psychological safety is another important aspect which involves an environment and culture in which **'speaking up'** on any topic is encouraged, expected, and rewarded. Being able to **'be yourself'** is another important aspect of emotional safety in your workplace.
- **Social connection and enjoyment**. Work can, and should, be a place where you can feel connected to at least some of your work colleagues and enjoy the experience of being at work.
- **Being valued, included, and respected.** Everyone should feel included and respected at work and if that is not the case then it is important to address this issue. As I pointed out in the first book, one of the best ways to be more valued by the leaders of your legal department and firm, and especially by your clients, is to become a T-Shaped Lawyer.

Everyone should regularly 'check in' on these factors themselves to ensure that nothing is unnecessarily hindering their efforts to thrive at work or in life. If you have a coach, they can help you in in this process and point you in the right direction to help address any issues.

Managers should also be on the lookout for these factors, especially those related to the workplace, for a variety of reasons.

Employers in many countries have legal responsibilities to provide healthy and safe work environments and to identify, and to promptly address, situations which may lead to wellness or wellbeing issues for employees.

From a business perspective, providing a healthy and safe workplace that supports, rather than detracts from, the wellness and wellbeing of those who work there, has many benefits including greater productivity, enhanced performance, increased job satisfaction and greater engagement.

Wellbeing and wellness are necessary conditions to thrive at work, but they are insufficient on their own. The other key aspect of the personal dimension is to understand yourself and all the things that make you the unique human that you are.

B. Understanding Yourself

Self-awareness should really be the starting point for any attempt to progress professionally[6] especially if you wish to transform to be a T-Shaped Lawyer. It is essential to wellness and wellbeing because you can't fix what you don't know is out of balance.

Self-awareness is also a crucial component of emotional intelligence, key to effective leadership, and vitally important to happiness and fulfilment. It is relevant, for example, in formulating your life and career goals, changing your mindset, addressing problems that may impact your career, identifying areas for professional and personal development, and monitoring any changes you try to make.

So, what is self-awareness?

Self-awareness is about understanding yourself; your feelings, needs, aspirations, preferences, failings, habits, and everything else that makes you the unique individual that you are.

Self-awareness is a vast topic that is covered extensively in books[7] and articles written by authors with more relevant qualifications than me. **For this book, I propose to just focus on a few general affective and cognitive areas of self-awareness** which are particularly relevant to your professional development as a lawyer and to the T-Shaped Lawyer Framework. These are as follows:

- **Feelings, emotions, and moods**. It is crucial to comprehend these affective factors for several reasons. Your decisions are often driven by emotions, which also influence the way you interact with others, how you feel physically and mentally, and your cognitive abilities including learning. A detailed discussion of these factors is beyond the scope of this book but there are many resources available to help you assess, change, and manage them including these references[8].
- **Mindsets and attitudes.** The way you perceive yourself and the world, together with any predisposition in relation to someone or something, can significantly influence your behaviours and your ability to learn. As such it is critical to

understand your mindsets and attitudes and to change these to the extent that they are hindering you from thriving at work. We will discuss some very specific mindsets relevant to being a T-Shaped Lawyer in Chapter 7.

- **Qualities**. Everyone has a range of human attributes that can either assist or frustrate your efforts to thrive at work. This topic will be discussed in some depth in Chapter 5 in relation to some very specific qualities relevant to being a T-Shaped Lawyer.
- **Purpose and motivations.** Everyone is motivated by different things in life and for some that can amount to a specific purpose even if you have not articulated it as such.

Have you ever stopped to reflect on your purpose in life? Simon Sinek calls it your 'Why'[9].

Having a clear sense of purpose or meaning in your life can be extremely helpful from both a personal and professional perspective[10]. It can, for example, inform your life and career decisions, help you to cope with unexpected and unwanted surprises and, ultimately, help you to lead a more fulfilling and happy life.

One useful exercise is to prepare a Purpose Statement or Why Statement for yourself. There are numerous online and other resources available to help you prepare such a statement[11], but here are a few general observations:

- Your purpose does not have to be world-changing, spiritual, or grandiose.

- You may have more than one purpose.
- The more granular it is, the more helpful it will be for you.
- It is not for marketing purposes. It is a reference point for you, but you may wish to share it with those you trust and value for their feedback.
- Your work might constitute a large part of your purpose, or it might not.
- Preparing a purpose statement should be done over time to allow for reflection.
- There are various techniques and tools to help you think about your purpose and translate it into words that typically involve you trying to answer questions such as:

    - *What is important to me?*
    - *What makes me happy and fulfilled*[12]*?*
    - *Do I want to impact the lives of others and if so who and how?*
    - *How do I want to behave?*
    - *What are my core values?*
    - *What do I want others to think of me and say about me?*

- It can be helpful to see examples of other purpose statements[13] but resist the urge to copy and paste. Your purpose statement is unlikely to be the same as anyone else.

A component of purpose, but also something that is worthy of reflection on its own, is *motivation*. What motivates or energises you?

There is an increasing amount of research suggesting that things like money and promotions are not the main motivators for most people. For example, Daniel Pinks, in his book *Drive: The Surprising Truth About What Motivates Us*[14], concludes that the main motivators for most people are:

- **autonomy**, or the desire to be self-directed.
- **mastery**, or the desire to keep improving at something that is important to you, and
- **purpose,** the opportunity to make a difference, ideally in an organisation that makes a difference.

Interestingly, these motivators are strikingly similar to the top three factors that, according to a recent US study[15], make lawyers happy - namely autonomy, mastery, and relatedness. In my experience working with thousands of lawyers, some other common motivators include diversity of experiences, belonging to a team you connect with, developing or 'growing' yourself, or helping others to thrive.

Because your motivations may change over time, it is a worthwhile exercise to regularly check your purpose and motivations. The key point to remember is that your purpose and motivations should align with your aspirations and your work, and they should inform important career and personal decisions.

- **Aspirations and vision**.

In my first book, I highlighted the crucial importance of individuals and teams having a vision and I proposed a very general vision for every corporate lawyer- to be a T-Shaped Lawyer. I encourage you to read that book if you have not already.

Rather than repeat what I wrote there, let me ask you a simple but revealing question that a surprising number of lawyers have not considered:

'What would you like to be doing 2, 5, 10 years from now?'

- Do you see yourself as a manager, a partner, or a general counsel in the future?
- Would you like to change from a legal role into a business role at some point?
- Do you want to work overseas or in another location?
- Would you like to work part time or as a contractor and have more time to do things outside of your work?
- Do you want to start your own business?
- Are you planning to leave the corporate legal industry to do something completely different?

Your answers to this question reveal **your aspirations – what you hope for**. Articulating your specific aspirations is a useful intermediate step to help you formulate **your professional vision – what type of professional do you want to become to achieve your aspirations.**

Your aspirations may well change over time. However, your professional vision, because it is a more high-level general idea, is less likely to change.

When you are considering this question, it is extremely important to bear in mind your purpose as discussed above. Your vision should align with your purpose and should help you to achieve your personal and professional aspirations.

If you do not currently have any professional aspirations or vision then you have, by default, chosen to continue your current professional path. I pointed out some of the implications of this choice in the first book.

One comment that I frequently hear from in-house lawyers is how difficult it is to get a promotion within their team. If promotion is important for you, and your path is blocked, then it maybe that you will have to leave your current employer to realise your aspirations. However, before you get to that point, it is worth exploring what lateral, as opposed to linear, career options and development opportunities are possible in your current organisation. For example:

- Is there a project that you could participate in that will broaden your skills and experience?
- Maybe you cannot directly *manage* people as soon as you would like but you may be able to *lead* one of these projects.
- Perhaps there are interesting opportunities for you to move into a role in another function in your organisation.

- There are an ever-increasing variety of new roles appearing in legal departments and firms, such as legal operations or technology-related roles, that you may be able to help create or move into.

Another key point to remember in this context is that whereas in the past sticking to a linear career path may have maximised your prospects of success in a legal career, now that is not necessarily so.

As Harvard Law School Professor David Wilkins highlights[16] *'It (the future for lawyers) is scary in the sense that there used to be very clear, easily identifiable career paths that you could follow. And if you played by the rules, you'd be fine. Well, a lot of those career trajectories are being disrupted, whether by technology, competition, globalization, or by the kinds of problems that lawyers are being asked to solve. All these changes are pushing law from a "fee for service" model," in which* ***clients bring lawyers "legal questions," and lawyers provide "legal answers"*** *which the client then implements, to what I've been calling an "integrated solutions model." In this model,* ***neither the contours of the problem nor the possible array of solutions is strictly "legal" or fully understood by either the client or the lawyer.*** *Instead,* ***lawyers work collaboratively with a broad range of professionals*** *to help clients refine their understanding of the problem and the potential array of solutions in ways that promote the client's ability to continue to make good decisions moving forward.'*

It is difficult to think of a better endorsement than that for being a T-Shaped Lawyer or, for that matter, the crucial importance of diversity of experience, capabilities, and work beyond the law.

If you do aspire to a general counsel role, to be a partner or to any other role in the corporate legal industry, one thing is clear. **Your technical legal skills and knowledge may have primarily helped you to where you are today, but they are unlikely to get you to where you want to go tomorrow.** Why is that so?

Generally, as highlighted in the first book[17], **what matters more for a promotion is not so much your legal skills but rather other things such as interpersonal and business skills, and the ability to do a range of business work.** The reasons for that are quite clear, although rarely articulated to younger lawyers.

First, there is typically more differentiation between lawyers in a team or firm based on their business prowess compared to their legal prowess.

Second, to be an effective manager or leader in your legal department or firm, depends less on your legal prowess and much more on other things including non-legal capabilities and experience.

Third, business clients will find it difficult to differentiate lawyers based on legal prowess but will definitely notice, value, and recognise business prowess.

Fourth, you will find that the more senior you become, the less law, and the more business, you do on a daily basis. Indeed, as I point out in The T-Shaped Lawyer Spectrum™ featured in the first book, many partners and general counsels spend most of their time doing business, not legal, work. For example:

- Partners in firms need to manage the business of the firm which includes a range of work such as strategic planning, cost management, budgeting, facilities management, attracting and retaining talent, people management, coaching, mentoring, business development, project management, technology acquisition and development.
- General counsels, and other senior in-house lawyers, also need to manage the business of the department and that involves a similar range of activities as listed above for partners. In addition, they also need to be part of business management teams and to participate in the business discussions there as an equal member of that team and not just as the lawyer.

Suffice it to say that **whatever your career aspirations may be, you will enhance your prospects by not just trying to be a better lawyer but also by broadening your development beyond legal technical skills and by doing non-legal work**. In other words, by becoming a different lawyer; a T-Shaped Lawyer.

If that is your vision, then the rest of this book will explain how the best way to achieve that vision is to follow the T-shaped Lawyer Framework. It is specifically designed for that purpose. That said, it will also be informative and helpful even if this is not your vision.

C. How to align 'your personal' with 'your professional'

While this book is about your professional development, it is crucial to align this with personal considerations such as those outlined above. Before I explain how I suggest that you do that through a specific multi-step process, it is worth making a few general comments:

- At risk of stating the obvious, it is essential to regularly taking time out of your busy life for feedback and self-reflection. This involves you being conscious of, and honest about, yourself and your feelings.
- Some people are quite self-aware and can self-assess and self-reflect on their own. However, for most, there is value in involving trusted friends, colleagues, managers, or coaches to help you in this process.
- **Your vision is THE key to thriving@work. It is your reference point on your journey. It is the crucial link between 'your personal' and 'your professional'.**

Below is an explanation of one process you can use to align 'your personal' with 'your professional' using The T-Shaped Lawyer vision as an example.

<u>The Thrive@Work Evaluation Process</u>

Step	Action
1. Define your Vision	Articulate your aspirations and define your professional vision. For example, to be a T-Shaped Lawyer.
2. Identify the key enablers	The key enablers to be a T-Shaped Lawyer are all the components of The Framework, especially The Businessperson Mindset, Business Partnering and Business Leadership.
3. Assess and prioritise the enablers	Assessment of each enabler, as explained in this book, is critical because it reveals the gap between your current capabilities and what you need to develop to achieve your vision.
4. Identify any blockers	Check for anything that may impede you achieving your vision including: • any Framework component • any personal factor mentioned above.
5. Map out your 'strategic' action plan and a series of goals	Prepare goals and a plan that identifies the steps you will take, and when you will take them, to develop the key enablers and to eliminate or minimise the blockers.

The Thrive@Work process is not a linear or one-time process. It should be done iteratively and regularly at least once a year. Also, blockers may arise from time to time that need to be addressed immediately.

Assessment is a crucial step in the process. There are a variety of different ways to conduct this assessment. These include specific assessments, such as those mentioned in this book, related to a particular component of the Framework[18] or a personal factor.

Most of you will likely have gained some insights into your general strengths and development areas from feedback from family and friends. You should also have received feedback from work colleagues and/or your manager, as part of your organisation's performance review process.

There are also several other general tools available to you to gain deeper insights into your strengths and development areas including the following:

- 360-degree feedback involving obtaining feedback from your peers, subordinates and superiors[19]
- Johari Window[20]
- Clifton Strengths assessment[21]
- Personality type assessments such as Myer Briggs[22]
- core values index assessment[23]
- character strengths assessment[24]
- emotional IQ assessment[25]

Many lawyers have a rather inflated impression of themselves and do not like to acknowledge that they are less than perfect. For example, I am frequently told by lawyers I encounter that they are a T-shaped Lawyer. Yet they typically have significant gaps measured against the T-Shaped Lawyer Assessment and they do far less client business work than they might think.

Whatever means you choose for assessment, it is important to gain a realistic understanding of your general strengths and development areas, and the vision-specific enablers and blockers.

It will be assumed that you wish to adopt The T-Shaped Lawyer vision and so the rest of this book will explain how you can develop your capabilities to realise that vision – to become a businessperson, not just a lawyer, and to provide business input and advice, not just legal advice, and to do business work, not just legal work, for the benefit of the business, not just the legal department or firm. That said, the Framework and this book will also be extremely informative and helpful even if this is not your vision.

CHAPTER 2

OVERVIEW OF THE T-SHAPED LAWYER FRAMEWORK

As explained in my first book, it is now generally accepted that lawyers need to develop and use non-legal skills and knowledge[26]. Now, almost everyone is speculating which new skills you need and typically referring to these as *soft* or *human* skills.

There are several problems with this type of speculation. Highlighting these problems provides context for the explanation of why the Framework is essential.

First, references to *human* skills are typically not skills at all, but rather qualities. Being precise about this terminology is more than semantics because how you develop and use a skill is completely different from how you develop and use a quality.

Second, references to *soft* implies that these skills are optional, lightweight, easy-to-learn or not as important as hard skills. Nothing could be further from the truth. In the first book I highlighted the growing body of evidence and opinion that so-called soft skills are at least as important for everyone as hard technical skills in getting a job and then succeeding in it[27]. This is especially true when you consider the increasing extent to which generative artificial intelligence will assume traditional legal work and that people will be increasingly valued on their ability to do what technology cannot do.

Third, skills are only one part of the equation; it is also essential to develop *mindsets, knowledge, qualities, and competencies* and to be precise about the meaning of each as explained in this book[28].

Finally, and perhaps most importantly, it is impossible to decide what new skills and other capabilities you need unless and until you first answer the questions:

- ***why do I need them?***
- ***how will I use them?***

It should be obvious that developing non-legal skills cannot just be to do legal work. However, that is the implication, and the consequence, if you do not give due consideration to these critical preliminary questions. **That is particularly problematic because, as you will soon discover, non-legal skills are not that relevant to doing legal work!**

That is why I deliberately chose to write the first book, before writing this second book. It encourages you to think about why you might need to change yourself and your work, and what you are seeking to achieve with such a change. It recommends that, to add more value for your clients and for other reasons mentioned in the book, **you should aspire to become a T-Shaped Lawyer – someone who is a businessperson, not just a lawyer, who provides business input and advice, not just legal advice, and does business work, not just legal work for the benefit of the business, not just your firm or department.** This vision is depicted in the graphic below.

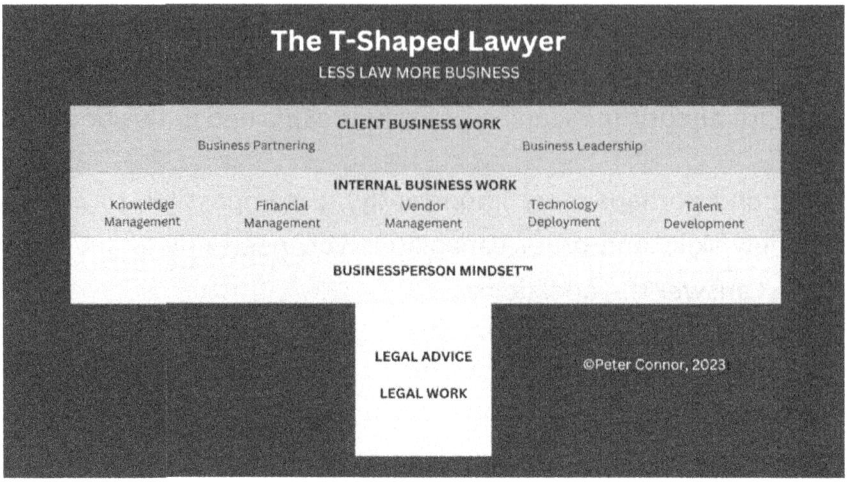

If you have not read the first book, then I highly recommend that you do that first. However, to briefly summarise some key points from the first book, as a corporate lawyer there are two broad categories of work that you can do, **legal work and business work.** A traditional I-shaped lawyer just does legal work, and a T-Shaped Lawyer is involved in both legal and business work.

It is crucial to break business work down into two subcategories – internal business work and client business work.

Internal business work, examples of which are shown above, is primarily for the benefit of the legal department or firm. Internal business work in most firms and legal department is primarily done not by lawyers but by legal operations and other professionals who are often not lawyers. That said, any lawyer who is, or aspires to be, in a senior position in a firm or legal department needs to understand and support internal business work.

Client business work, by contrast, is primarily for the benefit of the client. Client business work involves helping to solve or prevent business problems and to create or optimise business opportunities. Client business work can be done in conjunction with legal work but can also be done without any legal work involved at all. It can be broken down into two further subcategories - business partnering and business leadership. **Business partnering** involves the provision of business input and advice, over and above any legal advice. **Business leadership** involves doing more than just providing business input and advice and devoting more time on doing business work that often involves a project.

It is imperative to keep the distinction between these different types of work front of mind when you plan your professional development and answer those questions of *'why do I need new capabilities'* and *'how will I use them'*.

What skill or other capability you need, how you develop it, and how you use it, will depend entirely on whether you are talking about doing legal work, internal business work or client business work.

The first step is to decide what type of lawyer you want to be and what type of work you propose to do.

If you choose to be an I-shaped lawyer and just focus on legal work, then:

- of course, you need legal skills and legal knowledge.

- you do not need to develop non-legal skills[29], such as those in the Framework, because they are not that relevant to legal work.
- qualities, non-legal competencies, and non-legal knowledge, such as those in the Framework, are helpful but less crucial to doing legal work.
- the Framework mindsets are not essential to doing legal work.

If, on the other hand, you wish to become a T-Shaped Lawyer, or for that matter any other type of professional working in a firm or legal department, then all the Framework components will help you to do internal and client business work.

On the assumption that you do wish to be a T-Shaped Lawyer, what do you need to develop to be more capable of doing or supporting these different types of business work? Unfortunately, there is no 'silver bullet' or magic skill that is going to make all the difference for you.

A. <u>Why is the Framework necessary?</u>

If you are serious about transforming yourself to become a T-Shaped Lawyer so that you can do business work not just legal work, then you need a range of very different and specific things. The T-Shaped Lawyer Framework is an attempt to capture this range of things which includes non-legal skills but so much more as shown in this graphic in section C of this chapter below.

A framework is important because otherwise you will end up making a random selection of developmental areas that are unlikely to produce the results you are seeking.

The other benefit of a framework is that it provides a structured ,more strategic, approach for your professional development. It is the equivalent of a guidebook for your professional development journey that explains the relationships between different components and the different ways to develop and to use each of these. In the absence of a framework, you may learn about a component but not make the best use of it in conjunction with other components.

There are many other benefits of a framework such as the T-Shaped Lawyer Framework including that it:

- acts as a checkpoint against which you can assess yourself.
- can be used to diagnose any individual and team issues.
- provides a common language for professional development within a legal department or firm.
- can inform hiring, performance reviews, recognition, team-wide training programs etc.

There is another very important reason why the Framework is so necessary. It relates to the unique way that adults learn effectively.

B. Transformative Learning Theory

More and more organisations and individuals are embracing re-skilling and lifelong learning. However, because the goal of learning in the context of professional development is not just to acquire information, it is important that the way you learn is effective. Otherwise, the outcomes from learning are suboptimal.

Learning as an adult is different to learning as a child. There are many different theories for effective adult learning. A comprehensive coverage of these theories is beyond the scope of this book. However, I will briefly mention one theory, ***Transformative Learning***, that was developed by Jack Mezirow[30] specifically for situations where transformative change is your objective. This theory provides a highly regarded scientific basis for the approach taken in this book. It validates the crucial importance of clearly articulating 'the why' and 'the what' change you are seeking before deciding 'how' to achieve that change.

Transformative Learning theory posits that learning experiences will be more effective for adults if they are grounded in meaning and purpose. **There is no better way to incorporate meaning and purpose into learning than to use it specifically for a transformative change of the type proposed in my first book – to transform from i-shaped lawyers to become T-Shaped Lawyers.**

There are ten steps involved in the application of Transformative Learning Theory. These steps and the natural connection with the T-Shaped Lawyer transformation is briefly described below:

1. **Experiencing a disorienting dilemma where someone realises that something they thought or believed in the**

past may not be applicable in the future. The discontinuous changing landscape for lawyers as mentioned in the Chapter 1 of the first book and especially the relentless encroachment of generative artificial intelligence on traditional legal work should give rise to that sort of 'Aha moment' for most lawyers.

2. **Undergoing self-examination**. Reflecting on your frustrations and aspirations as explained in Chapter 2 of the first book and Chapter 1 of this book.
3. **Critically assessing assumptions**. Both my books encourage you to re-assess many assumptions including:
    - whether what got you where you are today will get you to where you want to go in the future.
    - whether technology is all important or whether you need to increase your focus on human transformation – what work you do and your capabilities to do new work.
    - whether your change objective should be to just improve to be a better lawyer, or to transform to be a different lawyer.
    - whether the name of the game is the efficient delivery of legal services or something different as indicated in my first book.
    - your current and future role as a lawyer.
    - the needs of your clients and their expectations of you and whether this is confined to just legal advice and legal work or something more than that.
    - the meaning of legal work.
    - the level of risk the business is prepared to take.

- what type of work really matters to your clients and to your manager in a firm or legal department.
- your capability to be something more than just a lawyer - a businessperson who can do different types of business work.
- your professional vision.
- the skills and other capabilities you need now and into the future.

4. **Recognising a connection between your dilemma and the process of transformation**. Understanding that the default vision of trying to improve to be a better lawyer may not suffice and that you may need a new direction which involves a transformation to be a different lawyer, a T-Shaped Lawyer, realise your aspirations and address your frustrations.
5. **Exploring options for new roles, relationships, and actions**. As outlined in the first book, considering different alternative visions including The T-Shaped Lawyer vision and the change that will have on your role, your relationships with your clients and on your work.
6. **Planning a course of action.** Using the T-Shaped Lawyer Framework as the basis for your professional development plan as outlined in this book together with a Work Rationalisation™ plan[31] to change your current work.
7. **Acquiring knowledge or skills for implementing these plans.** Executing the professional development plan to develop the Framework skills and knowledge together with the mindsets, competencies, and qualities.

8. **Exploring and trying out new roles**. Trying out being a T-Shaped Lawyer by starting with business partnering and looking for business leadership opportunities.
9. **Building competence and self-confidence in new roles and relationships.** Over time increasing the frequency and changing the style of business partnering and business leadership. Using the Businessperson Mindset to help that evolution and to reposition yourself with your clients as more than 'just a lawyer'.
10. **Integrating the changes into your life.** What starts out as something that you consciously focus on changing, will at some point just become 'the way you work' and 'who you are'; a T-Shaped Lawyer - a businessperson, not just a lawyer, who provides business input and advice, not just legal advice, and does business work, not just legal work, for the benefit of clients, not just the legal department or firm.

The implication of The T-Shaped Lawyer vision and Framework being consistent with Transformative Learning Theory is that it provides a purpose and meaning to your learning. In simple terms you are learning for a specific transformative purpose, to become a T-Shaped Lawyer. That means any development based on the Framework is likely to be significantly more effective than if there was no such context.

C. What is included in the Framework and why?

Below is a graphic that provides a snapshot of the five key Framework dimensions and the components in each dimension.

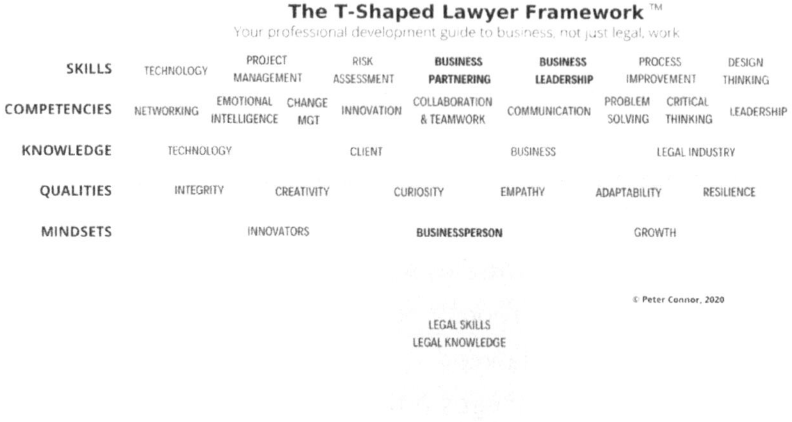

At first glance the Framework can appear a bit overwhelming. The way I propose to explain it to you in this book is as follows:

- Start, in this chapter, with a high-level overview of the Framework.
- Answer, later in this chapter, some common questions about the Framework.
- Dive deeper, in separate and subsequent chapters, into each of the 5 dimensions and the components of each dimension.
- In the final chapter, explain how to apply the Framework as individuals and as leaders of legal departments and firms.

To start the overview of the Framework, it is worth explaining that the selection of components is based on my own personal experience working as a corporate lawyer for more than 25 years around the world. Specifically, I reflected on what enabled me to become more than just a lawyer and to do internal and client business work in addition to legal work. That is how I came up with the initial list of components.

Since then, over the last 9 years, I have refined and tested the Framework with clients such as Rajah Tann Asia and in workshops with thousands of corporate lawyers over the world. I have also incorporated research and other expert opinions to substantiate or reinforce my own ideas and theories.

As much as everyone in the corporate legal industry is talking about the need for non-legal skills, it became obvious to me that there is a lot more to it than just skills. **Specifically, what is needed to be a T-Shaped Lawyer is a combination of *skills, competencies, mindsets, qualities, and knowledge.*** Having a workable taxonomy is important to plan and execute your professional development in an effective way.

What is the distinction between these five different dimensions?

Somewhat surprisingly, there is no consensus in human resource management theory on this taxonomy.

Below is my attempt to classify specific component areas into what I believe to be the main categories or, as I call them, dimensions. It is not intended to be definitive nor exhaustive and I fully expect that some of you will take issue with parts of this taxonomy and may wish to use an alternative taxonomy.

For this book, I shall be using the following definitions and taxonomy:

- **Skills – expertise needed to achieve a work outcome in a specific context.**

Examples: *legal skills* like contract drafting or legal research and *non-legal skills* like process improvement, design thinking and project management.

Skills are learned, can be developed, and are applied in specific contexts. There are, of course, skills that are relevant beyond your work context. In this book I am referring only to some specific work-related skills most relevant to being a T-Shaped Lawyer.

- **Competencies – abilities that help you to be successful in a range of tasks or jobs.**

Examples: *behavioural competencies* such as teamwork, collaboration, communication, critical thinking, and problem solving and *technical competencies* such as contract management, legal operations, or intellectual property enforcement.

The Framework focuses only on behavioural competencies because, unlike technical competencies, they are more important to doing business work. Behavioural competencies are learned and can be used by anyone in the organisation in a wide variety of contexts. A competency typically involves a combination of skills, knowledge, and qualities.

- **Qualities – personal attributes that are demonstrated independent of context.**

Examples: empathy, creativity, integrity, curiosity, resilience, and adaptability.

Qualities are *innate* in the sense that everyone has them to some degree. However, like muscles, they may be more, or less, obvious depending on the extent to which they are used. You can, to some extent, enhance and develop these attributes. They become part of who you are as a human being and, as such, you can use them in your work but, also, in other aspects of your life. Qualities are sometimes referred to as 'human skills' but this description is not only inaccurate it is also unhelpful because skills are developed and used in different ways to qualities.

- **Knowledge – understanding of, or information about, a subject gained through experience or education.**

Examples: *legal knowledge* such as the data protection laws of a particular region*; business knowledge* such as the business model and financial plans of an organisation*; general knowledge* such as the cultural habits and traditions in a particular country.

Knowledge is increasingly easy to obtain, and share, because of the internet and a range of technology solutions and online services especially since the emergence of generative artificial intelligence.

- **Mindsets – set of beliefs that shape how you make sense of yourself and the world.**

Example – a beginner's mindset.

If qualities are what you are actually like, then mindsets are how you perceive yourself and the world. As such it is important to be aware of your mindsets and the extent to which they frame the way you think and behave.

Is the distinction between these five dimensions important?

You may think that it doesn't really matter if someone calls a quality a skill or is otherwise imprecise when it comes to the terminology used for professional development. However, it matters greatly.

The way you develop each component is different and the way you use each component is different. Also, the components of the Framework have very different impacts on your ability to do legal and business work. For example:

- **Mindsets** are the foundational basis for re-skilling, without which you may gain little from trying to develop new **skills** and **competencies.**
- A **quality** or a **behavioural competency** generally takes a long time to develop to a point where it is noticeable to you and others. Most **skills,** on the other hand, can be learnt, at least to a basic level, and applied more immediately.
- **Skills,** by definition, allow you to achieve specific outcomes at work, whereas **qualities and behavioural competencies** do not.
- **Qualities** and **behavioural competencies** underlie the ability to learn and apply **skills**.
- There is a lot of interdependence, and multiple interconnections, between each of the dimensions and the components in each dimension. For example, **knowledge** is

critical to enhance your **creativity quality** which is a core component, along with **empathy** and **the behavioural competence of collaboration,** in the **skill of Design Thinking.**

Just to be clear, I am not implying that qualities and behavioural competencies are less important or not worth investing in. In general, however, they tend to be more helpful to you professionally when developed and used in conjunction with skills to produce specific outcomes. For example, being more empathetic may not result in any noticeable difference at work unless and until that quality is utilised in combination with a skill such as Design Thinking or when drafting a more customer-centric contract.

You will also notice that I have not identified in the Framework, or covered in this book, the vertical dimension – legal skills and legal knowledge. That is because this is an area that, unlike the horizontal dimension, most lawyers understand well and there are many existing resources available. It is also because this book is focused primarily on how to be better at client and internal business work, and legal skills and knowledge are not relevant for that purpose. That said, when I help clients build out the Framework for professional development of their team or firm, we do of course include components on this vertical dimension.

Each one of you will have unique needs and limited time to develop these capabilities. You want to get the maximum return on your investment of time and money. The taxonomy allows you to better understand the role each component plays and to appropriately focus your training and development, and your use of each component, as explained throughout the book.

D. Answering common questions about the Framework

In the final chapter of the book, I will answer questions specifically related to how to apply the Framework at an individual and department and firm level. However, for now, I will answer a few general questions that I know from experience you may want to understand better before we dive into the detail of each of the components of the Framework.

There are a lot of components in the Framework. Am I expected to develop all these even if I am a junior lawyer?

The short answer is yes. However, it is important to remember that a T-Shaped Lawyer is a legal expert business generalist. That means that, even in the long term, the overall aim of the Framework is **not** necessarily for you to become an expert in any of the Framework component areas.

Rather, the aim for everyone, irrespective of seniority or role, is to develop as quickly as possible what I refer to as a base level of understanding of each of the component areas. That does not involve much of a time commitment. Reading this book will provide that level of understanding. The reason why that is important is because it means that everyone in a legal department or firm is aligned to support, and to the extent possible participate in, both internal and client business work.

When I help clients roll out the Framework for a team, we define a range of levels for each skill and competency component from base level up to expert. I encourage each team to have higher levels of expertise for all these components at a team level. However, individuals typically develop higher levels over time for any such component only as and when there is a need or interest.

Are some Framework components more important than others? How do I decide which ones to focus on?

There are some components that are more important than other areas for every lawyer. For example, to be a T-Shaped Lawyer the Businessperson Mindset, business partnering, and business leadership are key and worthy of immediate focus. Otherwise, going through the assessment process will reveal which components are especially important for you to thrive at work. That said, every lawyer should understand every component of the Framework at least to a basic level.

What about interpersonal skills? Why are they not identified in the Framework?

People often refer to 'interpersonal skills' and rightly emphasise how important they are to individual contributors and, especially, to managers and leaders. What are interpersonal skills?

Interpersonal skills are what you need to communicate and interact effectively with people. Clearly that is crucial to you thriving at work and in life. The reason that I did not specifically identify interpersonal skills in the Framework is because they are really a combination of different Framework skills, competencies, and qualities such as communication, networking, emotional intelligence, leadership, teamwork, and collaboration. If you develop and use these Framework components, you will be enhancing your interpersonal skills.

Can I add other components to the Framework?

As mentioned earlier, the components I have selected for the Framework are the ones that I found from my own experience to be the most relevant to doing client business work. I have not included components areas relevant to just legal work or just internal business work. When I work with clients to adapt the Framework for their specific needs, we typically do include some additional components for these other purposes. You should feel free to do so also.

Can I use the Framework even if others in my department or firm do not?

Obviously, it is preferable if your legal department or firm does use the Framework for their professional development programs or at least supports you using it. However, there is usually nothing to stop you from using the Framework for your own professional development and from getting involved in internal business work and doing client business work as explained in my first book. In the unlikely case where you are prevented from doing so then it might be time to consider if your department or firm is the right place for you to work.

Do I need to develop these Framework capabilities before I can start doing business work?

Absolutely not. As explained in the first book, you can, and should, start offering business input and doing business work right now at the same time as you develop these capabilities.

Now that you have a general understanding of the T-Shaped Lawyer Framework it is time to dive deeper into the individual components of the framework in the following chapters starting with the T-Shaped Lawyer skills.

CHAPTER 3

T-SHAPED LAWYER SKILLS

Skills are crucial 'assets' for you to develop because skills, unlike competencies, qualities, and knowledge, allow you to achieve specific outcomes in your work. In other words, skills help you to make a more immediate and noticeable impact in your work.

Every lawyer will, to varying degrees, have developed a range of **legal skills** such as legal research, contract drafting, legal analysis and negotiation[32]. However, most lawyers have not developed many **non-legal work skills**. That is probably because, **if you are focussed on doing legal work, non-legal skills are not as relevant for that purpose as they are to doing business work.**

The specific non-legal skills that I have selected for the T-Shaped Lawyer Framework were chosen precisely because they are primarily of use for internal and client business work.

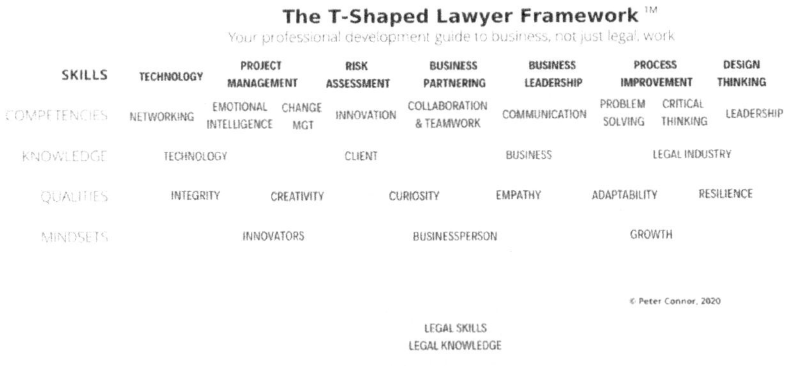

Since 2015 there has been an increasing number of articles and books written about the importance of non-legal skills such as:

- Legal design
- Legal project management
- Legal process improvement
- Legal technology development and deployment

The fact that the word 'Legal' is used as a prefix to describe these skills tells you something although this is almost never made clear. **It tells you that the skill is mostly being used for internal business work or, in some cases[33], legal work. It tells you that they are NOT referring to using the skill to do client business work.**

Why is that important?

First, although all lawyers should understand how to use these skills for internal business work, and for the few situations where they might be used for legal work, increasingly the application of these skills for this purpose will be done by legal operations and other professionals in your legal department or firm. As a lawyer, you will rarely need to use these skills for that purpose.

Second, as will be highlighted in the discussion in this chapter on each T-Shaped Lawyer skill, **using these skills for a different purpose - client business work offers enormous, largely untapped, scope for all lawyers to add value for clients through business leadership projects.**

I will briefly explain how each skill can be used for internal business work and, where applicable in relation to legal work. **However, the primary focus in this chapter will be on how to use each skill for client business work. That use scenario is rarely, if ever, covered in legal commentary. It is that use scenario that is most relevant to all lawyers. It is that use scenario where you can make the biggest impact for your clients.**

For each of the T-Shaped Lawyer non-legal skills (other than business partnering and business leadership which is covered in the first book) I will provide:

1. **a brief overview of the skill.**
2. **an explanation of how to use the skill for the different types of legal and business work.**
3. **some recommendations on how to develop the skill.**

A. Business Partnering and Business Leadership – the Super Skills

There are two primary and overarching non-legal skills - **business partnering and business leadership.**

The reason that I refer to these as the super skills is because:

- as explained in the first book, they are skills, but they also constitute the two types of client business work.
- the other T-Shaped Lawyer skills can and should be used to do either business partnering or business leadership.

Business partnering and business leadership are two ends of the spectrum of ways that lawyers can engage in **client business work. In other words, helping clients to prevent or solve business problems or create or optimise business opportunities.**

At a high-level, the main difference between business partnering and business leadership is that business partnering involves providing business input or advice. Business leadership involves dedicating more time to do business work that often is project based.

For a much more detailed explanation of what business partnering and business leadership is and how to develop your capabilities to use these skills to do client business work, I recommend that you read Chapters 5,6 and 7 of the first book.

B. Risk assessment and legal risk assessment

I like to ask those in my workshops whether risk assessment is an important part of their work as a lawyer. The standard response is '*of course, it is the primary thing we do*'. I then ask for a show of hands of those who have been trained on risk assessment. Typically, no hands go up.

It is ironic isn't it, that for something like risk assessment that is so important for every lawyer, there is virtually no guidance provided to you on how to use risk assessment?

Most managers assume that you know how to do it or that you will just learn it on the job, as they did. I also had that view when I was a general counsel until I realised that not everyone on my team had the same approach to risk assessment as I did.

For example, some lawyers:

- think that their role is to highlight just legal risk, not other risks.
- advise against doing something merely because a legal risk exists.
- do not like to make a recommendation because they believe that it is up to the business to make the decision.

When I do an exercise for my clients to point out the typically huge variation of risk assessment advice provided by lawyers, most partners of firms and general counsels are shocked. In effect there is very little quality control over the most fundamental thing that every firm or legal department does – legal risk assessment.

I mention this to highlight the importance of risk assessment as a skill and the imperative for the leaders of legal departments and firms to focus much more attention on developing this skill in a consistent manner through the department and firm.

1. What is risk assessment and legal risk assessment?

Legal risk assessment is the ability to identify, to assess, and to advise clients on legal risks such as regulatory risks or contract risks. **Risk assessment** is the same thing but in relation to all risks including legal risks but also other risks such as those shown below.

Business risks	Impact on employees, customers, distribution channels, or supply chain partners
Financial risks	Might involve revenue, ability to pay, price or cost variations
Technical risks	Technical dependencies, integration, adoption, update availability, ongoing maintenance, and support
Reputational risks	The way the public or your customers or shareholders will perceive a course of action even if it is legal
Legal risks	These include contractual risk, statutory risk, regulatory risk and, in some countries, causes of action under

	common law

The reason why I have included **risk assessment as a T-Shaped Lawyer skill is because if it is used for a full range of business risks, not just legal risks, then you are going above and beyond legal advice to provide business input and advice. You are using it for client business work.**

2. How to use risk assessment in your work

Risk assessment can be used in relation to:

- legal work, and
- internal business work and
- client business work.

The concept of using risk assessment to do legal work and provide legal advice requires no further explanation. It can also be used to assess and manage risks in relation to internal legal department or firm projects such as technology implementations or vendor transitions.

Using risk assessment in relation to client business work

Many lawyers when providing legal advice only identify legal risks and, often, only highlight the risk for the client without going much further.

Simply by expanding the scope of the risks beyond legal risks to other business risks, you can also use risk assessment to provide business advice and input. By expanding the breadth of the risks that you are considering you have the potential to add more value for your clients.

In addition to expanding the breadth, you can also expand the depth of your risk assessments. The graphic below shows how you can, and should, do that by going beyond the mere identification of risks. It maps out a process that I used myself when I worked as a lawyer and that I now use in my workshops with clients.

T-Shaped Lawyer Risk Assessment Checklist™

Scope	Legal + any other risk that you identify
Probability	Factual + Legal probability
Consequences	What the likely, not just theoretical, consequences and how likely
Enforcement	Who is likely to take action and how likely
Mitigation	How quick and inexpensive to mitigate
Alternatives	What other ways to achieve objectives with less risk
Rewards	How significant are the benefits from proceeding?
Recommendation	What do you think they should do?

The way to use this risk assessment process is to go through this checklist step-by-step. For significant matters it may be helpful to go through this list in your discussions with your clients and, in some cases, to even summarise your view on these points in writing. For less significant matters this could just be used by you as a quick mental checklist before you arrive at a conclusion and offer verbal advice.

When you use this skill in this way it will allow you to offer your clients business input and advice , in addition to any legal advice, about a transaction or matter.

It is relatively easy for **inhouse lawyers** to do this in most situations when they interact with business or functional executives even if there is no legal issue involved.

Lawyers working in law firms may not be engaged by clients unless there is a legal issue involved. However, whenever you are engaged you can follow the same process and either provide any business input directly to the business executives or, if that is not appropriate or possible, to the in-house lawyers involved. You may think that going beyond legal advice is not what your clients want. However, in fact failing to do that is one of the most common complaints in-house lawyers and business executives have about law firm lawyers - that you do not offer pragmatic business advice.

All lawyers will find that the better you become at doing this, the more business executives will come to you for your opinion at a much earlier stage then they would otherwise. **This is precisely how lawyers can become trusted advisors to their clients[34].**

You will rarely become a trusted advisor if all you do is provide legal risk assessments. However, if you also use risk assessment to provide insightful business input and advice then often clients will proactively contact you just to seek out your views on business decisions whether or not there are legal risks involved.

Below is a brief explanation of some key points for each step in the process:

- **Scope** – When your clients are making a business decision, they are considering all risks. Legal risks are only one type of risk and often not the most important consideration[35]. When you are conducting a risk assessment you should consider all risks, such as business, financial, technical, and reputational, not just legal risks. It is important to distinguish between each type of risk as you do your assessment under the following checklist points.
- **Probabilities** - There are two types of probability to consider in relation to all types of risk:
    - **factual probability** - how likely is it that something that could happen will happen? The more likely it is to happen the higher the risk and vice versa.
    - **legal probability** - how likely is it that, if something were to happen, it would give rise to a cause of action? That involves forming a view under the relevant laws. A simple way to do this is to rate the probability as either high, medium, or low.

Generally, the higher the probability of something happening, the more weight you need to give it in your risk assessment.

- **Consequences** - After you have determined the probability of something happening, the next thing is to consider the likely, as opposed to theoretical, consequences. You can also rate these as low, medium, or high impact and that can be adverse or positive. In relation to legal risks, the nature of the risk results in different potential consequences such as injunctions, damages, claims of various monetary values, criminal prosecution and personal liability of directors and officers. **Generally, the more likely it is that there will be an adverse and high impact, the less attractive it will be to proceed with the proposed course of action.**
- **Enforcement** - The next question to consider is how likely is it that someone will do something about it. For legal risks this typically means will someone, such as a regulator, contractual party, employee, or other stakeholder, take legal action against your client. The mere fact that a cause of action exists does not always mean that legal action is likely to follow. This might be the case, for example, where regulators in a certain country do not, as a matter of practice, take action in cases like the one you are considering. Alternatively, it may be that someone does not have the financial or other means to take action. **Generally, the less likely it is that someone will take action against your client, the more risk they might be willing to accept.**
- **Mitigation** - It is also important to consider what steps can be taken, either ahead of a risk event or afterwards, to mitigate risks to an acceptable level. **Generally, the easier and quicker it is to be able to take steps to mitigate the risk, the higher the level of risk your client may be willing to accept.**

- **Alternatives** - Helping your clients to clearly articulate their objectives can be an extremely useful contribution. One of the benefits of doing so is that it will sometimes help you see, and propose, alternatives that meet those objectives but with less risk.
- **Reward assessment** - Risk is just one consideration in a business decision. **When your business colleagues are making a decision, they weigh up the risk with the reward**.

  It follows that, to make a reasoned recommendation, you also need to be able to assess the reward or the business opportunity. To do that, you need to understand the business context of the decision being discussed. You need to think like a businessperson, not just a lawyer. Ask questions like:

  - *what is the potential financial or other return?*
  - *what are the costs involved?*
  - *does it involve a new, potentially important, customer?*
  - *will it open new markets or lead to further inventions?*
  - *how will your client deliver on its commitments?*
  - *what is the opportunity cost of not proceeding?*
- **Recommendation** - Often, especially when there are significant risks involved, your clients will appreciate your views on a matter or transaction. **They want to know '*what should we do?*'**.

  Some of you may be reluctant to offer a view because you may feel it is too risky for you to do so. But offering a view is where you can add more value over and above all the other steps in the checklist outlined above.

A crucial point to remember when you are making a recommendation is that the mere existence of a risk, even one with potentially significant consequences, does not necessarily mean that the right decision is not to proceed.

Your client is always willing to take some risk and the key is to understand what that appetite for risk is and then factor that into your assessment and recommendation. Clarifying your client's appetite for risk is one of the most important aspects of risk assessment because it sets the context for that assessment.

3. How to develop your risk assessment skills

The best way to develop your risk assessment capability is to practice it on a regular basis in a variety of different situations. For junior lawyers, this may involve shadowing a more senior lawyer or doing hypothetical scenarios together with your manager or other legal colleagues. The key point for all lawyers to remember when conducting a risk assessment is to use the checklist in a very deliberate and conscious way.

C. Technology and Legal Technology

In a world where technology is becoming more and more prevalent in our private and professional lives, data and digital skills become increasingly important for all lawyers.

However, this can be a confusing area. Technology is changing so constantly and so dramatically. Many commentators place so much emphasis on technology that you could be excused for thinking that it is the only thing that matters. This NOT the case as this book illustrates. Technology is a means to an end. It is NOT 'the end' as some would have you believe.

To compound the confusion, most of the focus in the corporate legal industry is on legal technology which, as I will explain, is only part of the picture.

The objective of this section of the book is to provide some much-needed clarity to the topic of technology related skills so that you can decide what type and level of digital and data skills you want to develop and utilise.

Before I do that, I should explain that I am not a tech nerd. I cannot code software. I can fix only the most basic technical problems with my laptop. Despite that, I worked successfully as a lawyer in the technology industry for about twenty-five years. In my last job, before starting AlternativelyLegal, I was Vice President of Technology for a compliance business, The Red Flag Group, where I managed a group of developers and data scientists to develop a range of compliance software.

The point of telling you this story is to highlight that you do not need to be a technology expert to be able to understand how technology can be used not just for yourself, but also for your firm or department (internal business work) and for the business of your client organisations (client business work). But to do that you will need to be digitally literate and to develop some basic digital and data skills as explained below.

At risk of stating the obvious, it is important for every lawyer to have at least a basic understanding of:

- technology in general
- the current and emerging popular technologies
- how to use the technologies most relevant to your work
- the key players in the technology industry and what products they supply.

Digital literacy is a language, and every lawyer must understand and speak that language to at least a basic level. I will discuss the basic technology knowledge you need in the chapter on knowledge later in the book.

Because there are so many different skills related to technology the explanation of each sub skill, and how to develop and use it, will be covered in the discussion of that sub skill.

Digital skills

I have developed my own classification of digital skills which I hope is helpful to simplify what can otherwise be a complex and confusing area for many lawyers. I classify the primary digital skills relevant to a lawyer as follows:

i. Using technology

The most fundamental skills involve the ability to use technology to help you in your work[36]. **In other words, these skills relate to how to use technology for legal work and for internal business work.**

In fact, in some states and countries, lawyers have a professional responsibility to develop and maintain a level of basic technology competence[37]. At a basic level, every lawyer should at least know about, and be able to use, general personal productivity technology, for example:

- word processing technology such as Microsoft Word or Google Docs
- presentation software such as Microsoft PowerPoint
- storage software such as Google Drive and OneDrive
- email systems such as Outlook and Gmail
- spreadsheet software such as Excel
- internet search tools such as Google
- video conference technology such as Zoom and Meets
- messaging software such as WhatsApp
- notes tools such as Evernote
- virtual workspace technology such as Slack
- task management such as Trello.

Lawyers also need to be competent with any relevant system used by your company, department, or firm for things such as accessing precedents, filing expense claims, authorisations, and deal or contract management. That technology may be general technology used by everyone in your company or firm or it may be LegalTech specifically for lawyers or others in the department or firm.

One relatively new technology that may be less familiar to most lawyers is using generative artificial intelligence technologies to augment your current work and to do business work. At the time of writing this book, ChatGPT has just been released. Although lawyers are still trying to fully understand this and other generative AI based products, it is obvious that every lawyer will need to learn how to use such technologies for their work.

Prompt engineering is one such skill that every lawyer needs to be able to use. It involves structuring text requests in such a way to yield optimal results from Large Language Models. A detailed discussion on this and other GenAI skills is beyond the scope of this book but here[38] are some resources to help you understand and enhance your abilities in this area.

Except for GenAI, the skills necessary to use technology for your traditional work are understood by most and if you want to develop these skills then there are a typically lots of internal and external resources available[39]. As a result, I do not intend to discuss these skills any further. Rather I will focus on other digital skills that are rarely discussed and which are important if you wish to be a T-Shaped Lawyer especially a senior one in your legal department or firm.

ii. Applying technology

Almost all the focus and discussion on technology in the corporate legal industry is on the first skill set – how it can be used by you to do your legal or internal business work more efficiently.

One different and very specific skill set that is rarely if ever discussed is the ability to leverage technology for your clients. **This is an example of client business work and I refer to it as applying technology.**

What is the skill of applying technology and how can you use it for your clients?

Applying technology is the ability to identify opportunities where your clients might benefit from a technology solution as a substitute for lawyers providing a service to the client. The most common generic use case is providing your clients with the documents and information they need without the need to involve you or any other lawyer. If you have read my first book, you will recall that this is an example of what I say is 'where the puck' is headed for the future of the corporate legal industry.

Examples of applying technology for clients include:

- self-service apps for review of marketing material or anti-corruption Travel and Expense approvals
- FAQ chatbots and custom ChatGPT sites

- contract systems that allow clients to use a template to complete a contract and send it to their customer.

In my view, applying technology is the most interesting of all the digital skills and one that is central to the T-Shaped Lawyer vision. Why? Because if the whole point of being a T-Shaped Lawyer is to add more value for your clients, as explained in my first book, then applying technology for clients is far more relevant, and offers far more potential to add value, than just using technology for yourself, the legal department, or the firm.

I first wrote about this topic, and its relevance to law firms and legal departments, in my article *'Will law firms become software companies[40]'*. What I was trying to convey with that article was that firms, and legal departments, need to think not just about how technology can help them, but how can technology be used to help clients[41].

There is a lot I could say on applying technology but, for the purpose of explaining this skill for all lawyers in this book, here are a few general comments:

- I am not suggesting that lawyers think about your client's technology needs in general. Rather, I am suggesting that, when you are thinking about how you can help the business of your clients in areas adjacent[42] to your work, consider whether that help may come in the form of a technology solution[43] rather than providing a service directly yourself.
- Richard Susskind, in the latest version of his book *Tomorrow's Lawyers[44]*, suggests that legal departments and firms adopt a

mission and strategies to design processes and systems to replace work currently done by lawyers and **to give clients the outcomes they need from the system and not from the lawyer.** The work to build these systems is an example of applying technology.

- in my article referred to above, I gave numerous examples of firms that have started to provide software to their clients and do not just use software internally. Likewise, progressive legal departments are increasingly arranging for the business to have access to a range of software from chatbots to contract management systems and other self-help tools.
- **one of the many attractions of developing this skill of applying technology is that it is always easier to obtain funding for technology, if you work in-house, when it is 'for the business' or, if you work for a firm, when it is 'for clients'**.
- the key to the skill of being able to apply technology is to have the Businessperson Mindset of a T-Shaped Lawyer, to broaden your knowledge of technology, to be able to identify where technology may provide the optimal solution to a particular problem or opportunity for the business, and then to leverage the other digital skills referred to below, together with your business leadership skills, to help facilitate a situation where your clients have access to and use the relevant technology.

iii. Assessing the need for technology

One of the most critical digital skills is the ability to properly assess whether you need new technology and, if so, what technology you need. The reason this skill is so critical is because:

- technology is not always the optimal solution for a problem as will be explained in the process improvement section below.
- new technology typically involves a significant investment in time and money and merely having it does not guarantee that it will be used.
- a failed technology implementation can have disastrous consequences for all concerned.

Being able to conduct a Technology Needs Assessment is undoubtedly an advanced skill, and a detailed explanation is beyond the scope of this book. Typically, you will want to engage an internal or external expert to help you with this crucial process. However, it is not something that you can abdicate entirely to an expert who may have their own biases. You want to be able to ask the right questions and to challenge any proposed solutions.

At a very basic level, when you assess the need for technology you should:

- start with clearly defining the problem or opportunity that you are trying to solve or exploit.
- assess the impact of this problem or opportunity with other problems or opportunities because you will need to prioritise any investment of time and money.
- examine root causes for any problem and whether a resource change or process improvement can address the situation to a satisfactory level.
- if a technology solution is the optimal choice for your problem or opportunity. If it is, then you have a few broad options:

- repurpose existing technology used in your company or firm.
- buy new technology or
- develop your own technology.

I am not suggesting that you as the lawyer needs to do the repurposing, the purchasing, or the development. However, knowing how to approach each of these options, and work with the appropriate internal or external resources, constitute important skills for a T-Shaped Lawyer. The best way to develop these skills is to get involved in technology projects in your legal department or firm.

iv. Repurposing technology

Before you look to purchase new technology, you should always ascertain what existing technologies are available in your company or firm and explore whether they can meet your technology needs or be adapted to do so. The best way to do that is to contact your IT department and ask them to help you in this exercise. They will usually be more than willing to help because it minimises, if not eliminates, integration, adoption and training issues that can arise with new technology.

Repurposing existing technology will almost always be cheaper than buying or making new technology. However, there will be cases where existing technology is not fit for purpose and then you need to consider the other options.

v. Developing technology

I am often asked by lawyers, *'should I learn to code'*?

My response to that question is always *'no'* because if you are interested in coding then you would have started learning already and you would not be asking me that question. If you are not interested in coding, then it is not necessary for you to learn how to code.

While being able to code is a useful skill to have, it is not an essential one for a lawyer because:

- increasingly there is a range of no-code software platforms available that allow anyone to quickly and easily configure the platform to develop apps that suit your needs rather than developing software from scratch. Examples include Neota Logic, Checkbox.ai, Josef and BRYTER.
- even in those cases where developing your own software is appropriate, as I mentioned above, it is not crucial that you are able to do the actual development yourself. Rather it is important that you understand the development process and can, if required, manage the development of technology by internal or external developers.

Managing the development of software is not an entry level skill and not necessarily for everyone. However, as a lawyer who has learnt how to do this, it is something you can learn over time with practise. There are numerous resources available to help you better understand the software development process[45]. However, the best way to learn is to get involved in a software development project in your legal department, company, or firm. At the same time, you will typically gain exposure to project management techniques.

vi. Buying technology

Although developing your own software may be an option in some cases, currently if you need technology and your existing systems are not fit-for-purpose, acquiring a new technology solution will often be the best option.

Technology procurement is a specialist skill and often larger companies and firms will have procurement experts who can assist you in any procurement project. However, as a T-Shaped Lawyer, it is helpful to develop a level of competence in this skill. This is especially important if you are, or aspire to be, a leader in your department or firm because ideally you want to be able to drive, or at least manage, any procurement project to ensure that it achieves the desired objectives.

To be proficient at managing a technology procurement involves a broad and current knowledge of technology, a topic that will be covered briefly in the knowledge chapter later in the book. It also involves several sub-skills such as:

- being able to work collaboratively with technology vendors and your IT department, understanding their biases and, at the same time, being able to leverage their knowledge and expertise.
- the ability to make the business case for budget for the technology procurement.

- project management of the procurement.

One organisation that is extremely helpful to lawyers, especially in-house lawyers, to assist in procurement of legal technology and legal services is the *Buying Legal Council*[46]. They have an extensive range of resources available to help you better understand the procurement process. Again, the best way to develop this skill is to get involved in technology procurements in your legal department or firm.

vii. Implementing technology

It is one thing to acquire or develop new technology, it is quite another thing for that technology to be used the way you had planned. Many technology projects fail because insufficient consideration is given to the practicalities of implementation.

The key things to consider are set out in this table below.

Integration	A stand-alone system is of far less value to a firm or company than a technology solution that integrates with other existing technology systems. That is because data from one system can feed into, and be used in, the other system. Typically, that requires the new system to have Application Programming Interfaces (APIs) that allow that system to connect to the existing systems. **Requirement**: You need to fully understand whether this is the case and, if not, what can be done to effect

	integration.
Adoption	The whole point of new technology is for others to use it. However, technology projects, especially those in the legal industry, often fail because those who are supposed to use it, do not do so. **Requirement**: The key to successful adoption of new technology is to follow a change management process as part of the project and to communicate regularly and effectively to all stakeholders involved.
Training	Users must be trained on the new system in time for the expected launch and must be easily able to seek support and guidance on how to use it effectively. **Requirement**: You must include system training into your project planning.

Again, you do not need to be an expert in the technicalities of technology implementation. However, it is important, at least, to have a level of understanding and competence to ask the right questions of the experts assisting you with your technology projects.

Data Skills

Data is relevant to legal departments and law firms in many ways. For example, **Knowledge management** is essentially the capture, storage, and retrieval of different types of data generated by lawyers in the department or firm, including documents, opinions, research etc. **Operational data** is another key area of data which involves capturing data on the operations of a legal department or a firm such as where lawyers spend their time and their money.

There are various data skills relevant to these and other examples of data in legal department and firms including:

- understanding the importance of **data quality** and how to enhance it.
- **data visualisation** – the ability to display data in ways that others can easily understand.
- **core data management skills** including the security of and accessibility to stored data.
- the ability to use data to **support decisions** and actions, and
- **data analytics** - the ability to analyse, extrapolate and correlate knowledge about data in new contexts and unforeseen and novel situations.

Not every lawyer necessarily needs to be an expert in these skills, especially in larger departments and firms that have staff that are experienced in these areas. However, like many of the T-Shaped Lawyer skills, it is extremely helpful if you aspire to a leadership position, to develop a basic level of competence in these skills.

As with all the Framework skills, it is important for a T-Shaped Lawyer to be able to use data skills for the business, not just for the legal department or firm. For example, when it comes to risk assessment of a transaction or matter, try to obtain, and analyse data on actual, as opposed to theoretical, risks in the business. This might inform a very different approach.

Also remember that data is the 'language' of your clients – the business. To be able to speak in the language of the business, it is important for all corporate lawyers to understand numbers and use them wherever relevant. At a minimum that involves understanding the key financial metrics for your company, legal department or firm and being able to incorporate references to numbers in your communications and presentations wherever possible.

You may think, because my books are about human, not digital, transformation, that I do not place much importance on technology. Nothing could be further from the truth. I emphasise human transformation because there is so little focus on it compared with digital transformation and because it is important to understand that technology is a means to an end, not the end itself. That said, you cannot be a true T-Shaped Lawyer without an understanding of technology and without developing and utilising digital and data skills such as those that I have outlined above.

D. Process Improvement and Legal Process Improvement

In my experience, process improvement is one of the most helpful, yet under-rated and misunderstood, non-legal skills for a lawyer. There are many reasons for this such as:

- many of the problems that arise in firms, legal departments, and companies arise because of a lack of process, an inefficient process or one that is not being followed.
- improving these processes is a relatively simple and cost-effective way to solve these problems without the need for a technology solution.
- even if a technology solution is required, it is essential to first define and optimise the underlying processes.

1. What is process improvement and legal process improvement?

The first step in understanding process improvement is to understand what a process is, as explained below.

A basic process map

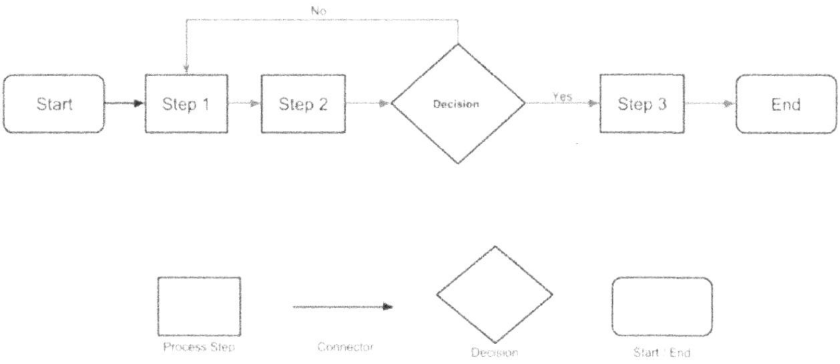

A process is any sequence of repeatable events with a start point, an output and a series of actions and decisions in between.

When we think of process, we generally associate it with a manufacturing production line. In such a process, parts are assembled during the process and the output is the finished product.

Every company, firm and legal department has many different processes, as explained below. Legal department and firm processes are known as '**legal processes**'[47]. Client processes are known as '**business processes**'.

The skill of process improvement involves the ability to define and streamline these processes primarily to make them more efficient.

If the relevant process is a client business process, then the skill is referred to as *process improvement* or *business process improvement*. If the relevant process is an internal legal department or law firm process, then the skill is referred to as *legal process improvement* or, sometimes, as *legal business process improvement*. This is explained in more detail below.

2. How to use process improvement in your work

Process improvement can be used in relation to:

- legal work
- internal business work, and
- client business work.

Using process improvement in relation to legal work

Although you may not think of it this way, a lot of legal work can be viewed as a process. Each matter or transaction may be unique. However, the steps that you might follow to do this work are often the same for every matter or transaction.

Examples: Potential legal work processes include:

- Litigation
- Mergers and acquisitions
- Trademark registrations
- Various contract related work.

Identifying these repeatable legal work processes, and then defining and optimising for efficiency and other reasons, is an effective application of process improvement.

Using process improvement for internal business work

In addition to legal work processes legal departments and firms have lots of internal business processes.

Examples: Internal business processes include:

- Hiring, assessing, developing, and terminating staff
- Strategic planning
- Work allocation
- Work intake and discharge
- Budgets, procurement, invoice payment
- Appointing, engaging, and managing law firms in the case of legal departments.

When you hear or read anything about process in the legal context, almost always the reference is to **legal processes** like those above. In these legal processes the people involved are usually all from the legal department or firm.

Streamlining these processes, often referred to as ***legal process improvement***, is a desirable thing to do. It can enhance efficiency, reduce time spent on low value work and help to save costs. Larger legal departments and firms often have specialists, such as legal operations professionals, to drive legal process improvement. However, every corporate lawyer should understand, and where appropriate initiate or support legal process improvement. **Legal process improvement is an example of internal business work.**

Using process improvement for client business work

Although it is rarely if ever mentioned in legal industry commentary, lawyers can also use process improvement to do client business work. This is, yet again, another example of how a T-Shaped Lawyer can look beyond the firm or legal department to help their clients in new ways in areas of the business adjacent to their work. This is an example of business leadership as explained in Chapter 7 of my first book.

Process, or the lack of it, is often at the heart of many problems that arise in companies. A lack of a documented process can result in inefficiencies, or other problems, because it means people can do the same thing in a different way each time. Even in organisations with well-defined processes, there can be problems arising from a flaw in the process or a problem in following the process.

Examples of problems with business processes include:

- It is taking too long to get through the process.
- It is taking up too much of your time or the time of other senior executives.
- It is causing other knock-on problems for the business.

But, surely, in that case it is up to the relevant function or part of the business to worry about these business processes? **Why should lawyers get involved?**

One reason is because often nobody else does get involved or because you or others in the legal department are adversely impacted by the situation. **Business process improvement also happens to be a terrific way for you to add more value for clients over and above doing legal work - the very essence of being a T-Shaped Lawyer.**

In the case of in-house lawyers, it is also a terrific way to limit the role and work of the lawyers to just those areas where it is necessary for legal involvement or where they can add value in the process. **It is a classic win/win scenario, like most business leadership work.**

If you are an in-house lawyer, then most of your work is part of a larger business process although you may not think about it in that way. For example:

- negotiating a sales contract is part of the broader Sales process of converting leads to sales.
- advising on an employee termination is part of the HR 'hire-to-fire' process.
- filing for a trademark or patent registration is part of broader marketing or product development processes.

The crucial advantage that in-house lawyers have is that they are often at the intersection of the company in so many different aspects of the business. This gives you unique insights and a rare opportunity to spot problems and opportunities to improve process. **However, you will only be able to capitalise on this unique position if you have the Businessperson Mindset, if you**

understand process improvement, and if you look beyond the immediate transaction or matter and consider the underlying forces at play.

Lawyers working in firms typically do not have the same advantage as in-house lawyers. However, again, if you are thinking beyond the immediate transaction or matter and consider the underlying reasons why a problem may have arisen, you can also ask questions and ascertain if there is a lack of process or one that is not working properly. If so, then you can point out this issue and offer to assist if you have the capability or resources in the firm to do so.

Now that you understand the different opportunities for you to use process improvement in relation to different types of processes, it is time to explain the different alternative ways that you can improve any of these processes.

Alternative process improvement methodologies

There are various alternative approaches to process improvement. Some of the most well-known methods include Six Sigma, Lean, Lean Six Sigma (a combination of the first two methods) and Process Mapping. Below is a brief description of each approach.

i. Six Sigma

Six Sigma was popularised by Motorola and General Electric in the 1980s. In simple terms, Six Sigma is about getting it right at least most (99.99966%) of the time. As such it is a methodology that is best suited for when it is critical to be accurate and to not make any mistakes. Six Sigma helps to achieve this level of output quality by identifying and removing the causes of defects (errors) and minimizing variability in a process.

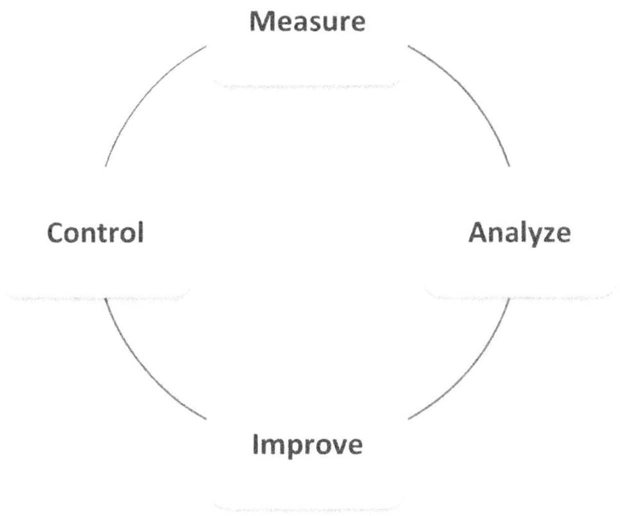

DMAIC

The steps for applying Six Sigma to an *existing* process are known as DMAIC and are shown above and can be summarised as follows:

- **D**efine customer needs and requirements.
- **M**easure the key aspects of the current process.
- **A**nalyse the data to ascertain the nature and cause of problems.
- **I**mprove the process and test and verify that this works.
- **C**ontrol the process so that errors don't reappear.

The steps involved in applying Six Sigma to a *new* process are known as DMADV. It involves the same first three steps as DMAIC, but the last two steps are as follows:

- **D**esign the new process based on the analysis in the previous step.
- **V**erify the design in a pilot then implement the new process.

Six Sigma is rarely used on its own in the legal context. Typically, it is used in conjunction with Lean thinking in an approach called Lean Six Sigma. Lean Six Sigma marries the waste-reduction principles of Lean with the quality-improvement efforts of Six Sigma.

ii. Lean

Lean thinking was initially developed at Toyota in Japan and has since been adopted and adapted for process improvement by many organisations in different industries around the world. Lean process improvement focuses on removing waste with the aim of leaving nothing else but activities that add value to the customer. It also helps to reduce cost and time.

<u>The 5 Principles of Lean</u>[48]

Lean thinking can be applied to process improvement and, as shown above, typically involves the following:

1. **Identify Value** - what does a customer value and how much it is willing to pay for it.

2. **Map the Value Stream** - all the steps across the entire *value stream* to produce the desired output.
3. **Create Flow** - by removing waste using the 8 types of waste as a reference. See graphic below.
4. **Establish Pull** - produce only what the customer *pulls* (needs): nothing else.
5. **Seek Perfection** - review the process regularly to remove waste in pursuit of perfection.

The 8 Wastes of Lean

Source: https://theleanway.net/The-8-Wastes-of-Lean accessed November 27, 2023.

Lean Six Sigma is increasingly used by progressive law firms[49] to enhance the quality of work and to reduce cost, time, and the variation in the way lawyers work. Lean Six Sigma is less commonly used in-house for a variety of reasons. However in-house departments are starting to use it for at least legal department process improvement when they have access to Lean Six Sigma internal or external expertise[50].

iii. Process Mapping

Many companies and firms use one of the above preferred process improvement approaches throughout the organisation. If this is the case, find those with experience at using it and leverage them to help train you or to help you use it. If not, then you can use a simple tool involving ***process mapping*** as shown below.

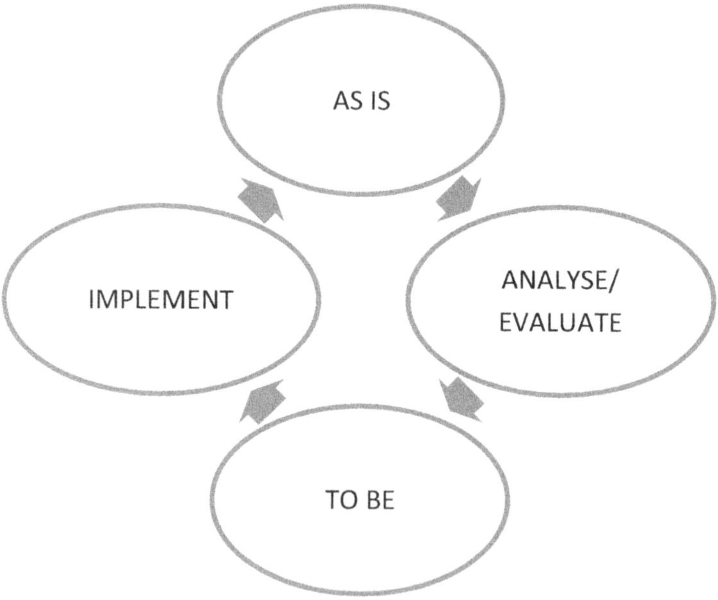

In process mapping, you start by documenting the current process – known as the ***'As Is'.*** This is typically done by assembling all those involved in a process and then meeting in a room and using post-it notes to document each step in the process as shown below.

After that meeting, someone then writes up the process either manually or using process software products and turns it into something like the example shown below. In this case the map can also be referred to as a *workflow diagram* because it literally shows the flow of work by different stakeholders involved in the process.

CONTINUOUS PROCESS IMPROVEMENT – 'AS IS' PROCESS MAP

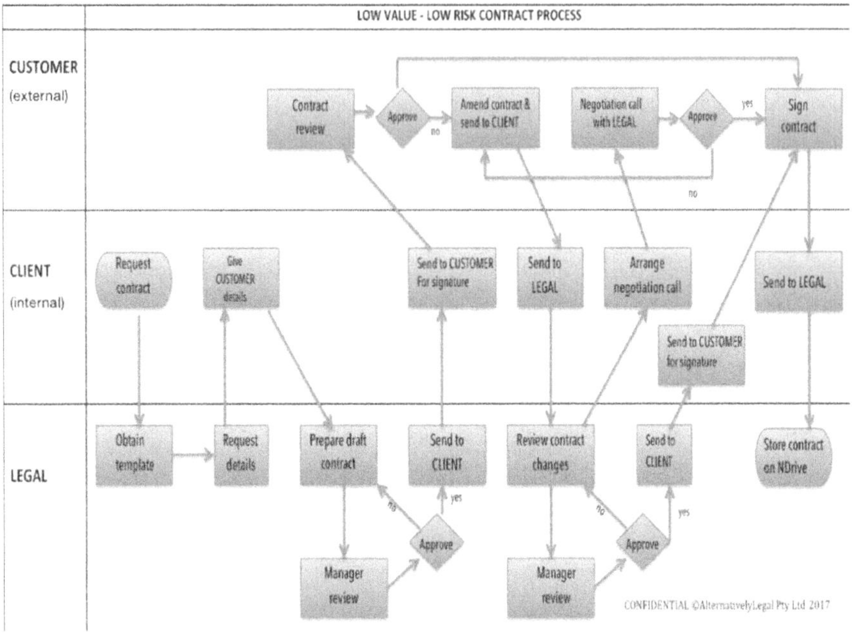

The next step in process mapping involves the same stakeholders, in a follow-on meeting, analysing the current process to look for opportunities to:

- eliminate unnecessary steps.
- speed up entire process.
- minimise meeting time and documentation.
- clarify responsibilities.
- minimise the legal department's involvement or delegate/outsource.
- assign tasks to business or other appropriate function.
- align with any relevant corporate approval process.

- automate manual steps.

After that step, the next task is to develop a new process that addresses these issues and that is known as the ***'To Be'*** process.

The final step is to implement the new process and then to continually monitor the process which is why this skill is often referred to as **continuous process improvement**. If the process, or parts of it, are to be automated, then it is referred to as **process or workflow automation** and there are various software platforms available for this purpose.

Whatever approach is adopted, the benefits of process improvement are many including enhancing efficiency, speeding up a process, spotting things for people to do and to stop doing, and allocating work to the appropriate person.

It is also critical to document and improve a process before you automate it. *'All the innovative software bells and whistles will not create business value if the underlying processes are broken[51]'.*

Example: In one case a legal department was about to adopt a new contract management platform for all their contracts. I used process improvement to first ascertain that, for almost half of the contracts, **we could eliminate the need for a paper contract altogether**. That significantly changed the scope of the automation project.

3. How to develop your process improvement skills

Having at least a basic competence in process improvement is important for all lawyers. At the very least, you want to be able to identify legal or business process improvement opportunities and know which internal or external experts to call in to help.

A simple way to start improving this skill is to try to identify the internal legal department processes and the underlying business processes that relate to your work. Then ask yourself:

- *have those processes been defined and documented somewhere?*
- *are these processes, or a lack of process definition, giving rise to any problems?*
- *do any of these processes relate to an upcoming automation project?*

Also, when you come across systemic repeated problems whether in your firm or legal department or in the client business, ask yourself whether there is an underlying process issue.

To the extent that you can, get involved in any process improvement initiatives. Also talk to any internal or external process experts. There are a multitude of resources for further study including these references in the endnotes[52].

E. Project Management and Legal Project Management (LPM)

Project management and **process improvement** are often, incorrectly, used interchangeably. They are related but require distinctly different skills, have different use cases, and involve different methodologies.

Example: The example below illustrates the difference.

If a company wants to acquire another company (ABC Ltd), the acquisition represents a project because that acquisition is a one-time undertaking. Achieving an optimal outcome in that acquisition requires collaboration and coordination between many different internal and external stakeholders to provide various deliverables on time and within budget. **Project management** refers to that coordination in relation to that specific project - the acquisition of ABC Ltd.

If the company were to undertake multiple acquisitions, then it could, and should, define an optimal step-by-step way to do these acquisitions in general. This would represent **a process**. Each acquisition may have its own unique considerations. However, it is possible and indeed desirable, to define an optimal process, with any necessary variations built in, to follow every time the company wants to acquire another business. Over time, it can and should refine that process to enhance efficiency and to minimise cost etc. This refinement represents **process improvement**.

There is a lot of material available for you to learn more about project management and this book is not intended to do more than give you a broad understanding of project management and provide you with some references for further study if you so desire.

1. What is Project Management and Legal Project Management?

'A project is any temporary endeavour with a definite beginning and end'[53]. Project Management is the planning and management of a project to achieve the project objectives. To be more specific, project management primarily **involves managing three critical interrelated aspects of any project - *scope, cost, and time***. This is known as **The Triple Constraint** as shown below.

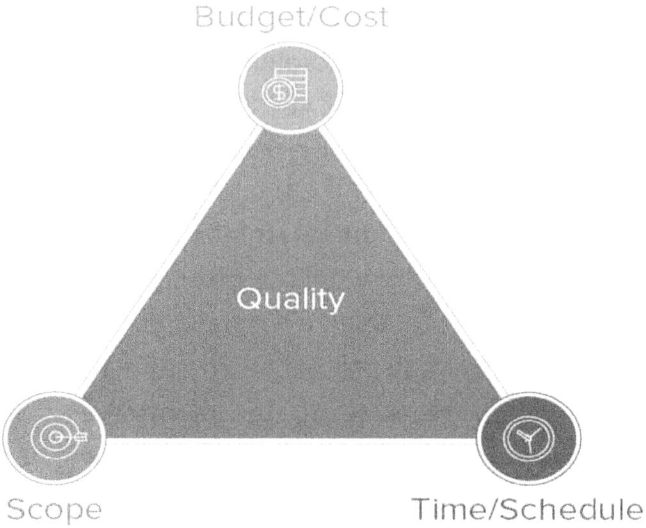

Source: https://www.smartsheet.com/triple-constraint-triangle-theory accessed November 29, 2023.

Adjusting any one of these three variables impacts the others. For example, an increase in scope of the project – say, from just acquiring ABC Ltd to integrating the business and people of ABC Ltd into the client company – will extend the time and likely the cost.

Managing the relationship between these three aspects is the key responsibility of the project manager. **Ultimately the success of any project is measured by whether the project team achieved the project goals within the agreed scope, cost, and time constraints.**

***Legal project management* is the same as project management, the only difference being that the projects relate solely to legal matters or internal legal department, or firm initiatives as opposed to client business initiatives.** This is explained further in the next section.

2. How to use project management in your work

Irrespective of whether we are talking about project management or legal project management, the approaches are similar.

Below are the typical phases of a project to give you a high-level insight into project management and to the terminology used. The extent to which these phases are followed rigorously will vary depending on the scale and complexity of the project and the type of organisation you work in.

The Phases of a Project

Phase 1 – Initiation: involves clarifying the objectives of the project and preparing a ***project charter*** that includes the ***business case*** showing financial and other benefits of the project and that identifies the key ***stakeholders*** - the project manager, the project sponsor, members of the project team and any other internal or external parties impacted by the project.

Phase 2 – Planning: involves several key steps such as:

- preparing the ***scope statement*** that describes the aims of the project, the ***deliverables*** to be produced during the project, an outline of the tasks involved to produce the deliverables, the measures of success and what constitutes closure of the project.
- preparing the ***Work Breakdown Structure (WBS)*** that splits the project into components to manage the project more easily. The WBS is often depicted on a ***Gantt Chart*** such as the one depicted below.

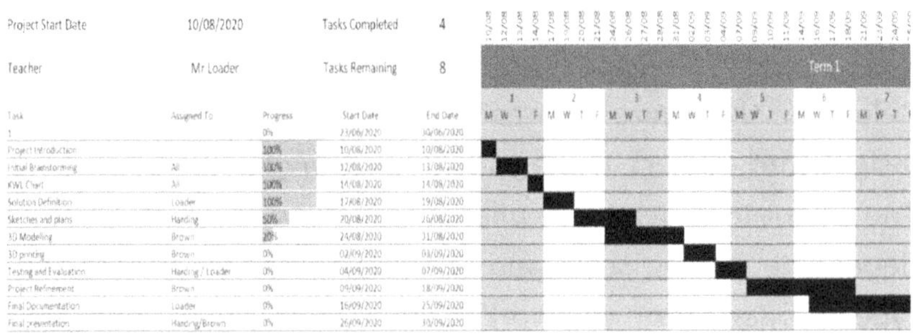

Source: https://stematpass.weebly.com/gantt-charts.html accessed November 29, 2023.

The Gantt Chart shows the tasks, who is responsible to complete the task and the target completion date plus any key deadlines known as ***milestones***. A milestone that is critical to the success of the project is said to be on the ***critical path***. Some tasks are standalone, but some are dependent on other tasks or events. These ***dependencies*** are explicitly highlighted and may constitute risks to project completion.

- planning for all the human and capital resources required to complete the project.
- identifying all the key risks to project completion
- preparing a plan for communicating progress to the key stakeholders during the project and for informing others at the appropriate time
- selecting a project management methodology - see below for an overview of popular methodologies.

Phase 3 – Execution: involves the kick-off meeting, project launch and ongoing work to complete the project in line with the Key Performance Indicators (KPIs) that will be used to measure performance of the project team. It involves regular team meetings and communications to key stakeholders.

Phase 4 - **Monitoring and Controlling:** involves tracking tasks and dealing with issues and risks as they arise or ahead of time. Control includes progress control, quality control and change control because of changes that inevitably arise during the project.

Phase 5 – Closing: involves producing deliverables and reports, obtaining sign-off from the project sponsors/stakeholders and conducting a post-mortem to learn from things that went well and not so well during the project.

There are different methodologies which can be used throughout these phases to manage a project. Some of the better-known ones are shown in the table below.

Method	Description
PMBOK	Project Management Book of Knowledge (PMBOK) is a set of guidelines published by the Project Management Institute (PMI). PMI also provides the popular PMP certification for project managers.
Prince2	Developed by the UK Government for IT projects and is now widely used for large scale projects. Prince2 is another popular certification for project managers.
Agile	Used especially in the technology world to manage software development in a way that is iterative, incremental, and responsive to changes during the project.
Waterfall	An alternative approach to Agile which follows a more linear process where you only move from one phase to another after the prior phase has been completed.
Scrum	Used to manage a project typically for smaller teams operating within a one- or two-week cycle and utilising short daily

	meetings to review and discuss progress.
Kanban	A visual approach to project management where the teams work is displayed on a board for discussion by the team.

Now that you have this general understanding of how to use project management, it is time to consider more specifically how you as a corporate lawyer can use project management in relation to your work.

Project management can be used in relation to:

- legal work, and
- internal business work, and
- client business work.

Using project management for legal work

Applying project management methodologies to legal work has been popular in most major law firms for some time and is also used in some legal departments. This use scenario is often referred to as Legal Project Management (LPM).

'LPM is the application of project management principles and practices to enhance the delivery of legal services' [54]. **LPM is really a fancy term for *matter or case management.***

The business of a law firm is all about delivering optimal outcomes on every matter for a client on time and within a budget. So, it is understandable that LPM is important in a law firm context.

The situation is different for most in-house lawyers. Typically, most of your work as an in-house lawyer would not justify applying project management methodologies because:

- you will not spend much time on a matter or transaction.
- the work is not that complex, or
- the work only involves you and one or two other colleagues.

However, if you do deal with many complex transactions or matters and you believe that utilising project management methodologies would be beneficial then you may wish to consider adopting project management in what is often referred to as **Matter Lifecycle Management** (MLM)[55].

Using project management for internal business work

The other context in which project management is relevant to legal departments and law firm is for internal business work. For example, legal operations or other professionals might use project management to manage projects such as:

- internal technology deployments
- spend control initiatives, and
- work rationalisation projects.

How to use project management to do business work

Like process improvement, a T-Shaped Lawyer will find opportunities to utilise project management **for business work**. If you have a basic understanding of project management and a

Businessperson Mindset you will, from time to time, recognise situations that could benefit from project management.

Example: any situation that requires several different business or functional executives at the client organisation to come together and work over a period of time to solve or prevent a business problem or to create or implement a business opportunity. For example, if you repeatedly notice that a problem arises such as lengthy internal delays or miscommunications; frequent customer, vendor, or channel partner dissatisfaction; or increasing regulatory attention. Often these situations are adjacent to your legal work, there is a lot at stake for the organisation and no-one else is stepping up to lead the effort.

If you initiate or play a central role in this effort, then that is classic business leadership as explained, with examples, in Chapter 7 of the first book. It was also explained there that you can show business leadership merely by pointing out to executives the need for project management and then knowing who to contact for assistance either inside or outside your company or firm. Alternatively, as an in-house lawyer if you understand project management, and you have the time, in some cases you can play the role of the project manager and enhance your contribution to your organisation.

3. How to develop your project management skills

Like all the T-Shaped Lawyer skills, your goal is not to become an expert in project management. Rather your aim is to, at least, understand project management sufficiently to be able to identify when your legal department, firm or your clients would benefit from project management. Ideally you would know which internal or external experts to bring in or, if no-one else steps up, be able to lead a project yourself.

In most countries there are a multitude of in-person and virtual courses offered on project management. There are also many resources for further reading such as these references[56].

That said, there is no substitute for learning by doing. Look for opportunities to get involved in projects in your firm, company, or legal department. Also speak to any internal or external project management experts to learn from them directly.

F. <u>Design Thinking and Legal Design</u>

Design Thinking and Legal Design have become increasingly popular in recent times in the legal industry and for very good reason; both can help to solve problems or improve products or services by involving 'the user' of a product or service.

Commentators in the legal industry tend to use the expressions Design Thinking and Legal Design interchangeably which can make it quite confusing for you. They share certain similarities but there are also some important differences in the way that they are used in practice as explained below.

1. What is Design Thinking and Legal Design?

Design Thinking is an iterative process involving regular user feedback that anyone can follow to quickly solve difficult problems and rapidly develop products and services that meet user's real, as opposed to perceived, needs.

Below are a few general comments about Design Thinking, it:

- is a form of ***Human Centred Design*** **(HCD)**. Human Centred Design is a way to solve problems or improve a product or service by focussing on humans at every stage of the process.
- 'the user' of a service or product is the human at the centre of this process.
- is not about thinking but rather about doing – trying something out.
- is not about just the appearance of something but rather about its usability and usefulness.

- relies on empathy, a T-Shaped Lawyer Framework quality covered later in the book.
- requires a particular mindset that is often referred to as a design mindset which essentially is a combination of the T-Shaped Lawyer mindsets.
- follows an iterative process as briefly explained below.

2. How to use Design Thinking in your work

The following is a brief overview of the design thinking process which explains how to use it. Typically, this whole process is conducted in a half-day or full-day workshop with all the key stakeholders and some users present. Often there is a lot of pre-work to ensure that the workshop can run efficiently and effectively.

The Design Thinking Process

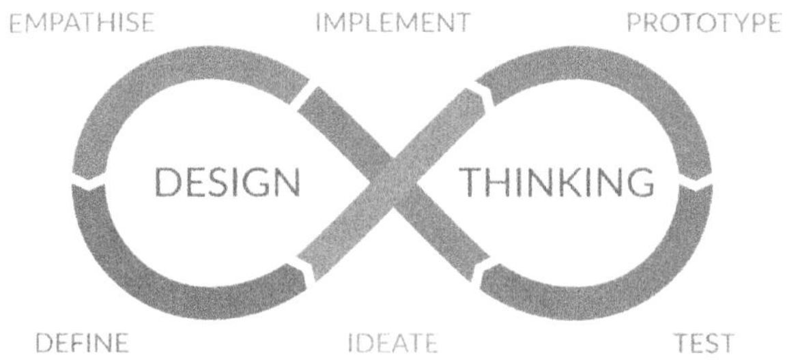

Source: https://www.system-concepts.com/insights/design-thinking-introduction/ accessed November 29, 2023.

Stage 1: Empathise - *Study and Understand Your Users' Needs*

At this stage, you seek to gain, through various research tools, an understanding of your users and the challenges they face from their perspective. **The user for a corporate lawyer will usually be the client but could also be your client's customers**. Empathy is crucial to a human-centered design process because it allows you to set aside your own assumptions and gain unique insight into users and their real needs.

Stage 2: Define - *Frame Your Users' Needs and Problems*

In this second stage, it is time to consolidate the information gathered during the Empathise stage. You then analyse your observations and synthesise them to define the core problems. These definitions are called problem statements which frame the next stage – ideation.

Stage 3: Ideate - *Challenge Assumptions and Create Ideas*

Now you are ready to generate ideas. The information from the first two phases means you can start to "think outside the box", look for alternative ways to view the problem and identify innovative solutions to the problem statement that you have created. There are a range of different ideation techniques.

Stage 4: Prototype - *Start to Create Solutions*

This is an experimental phase. The aim is to identify the best possible solution for each problem found. Then you should produce some inexpensive, scaled-down versions of the product or service to investigate the best ideas you have generated in the next stage.

Stage 5: Test—*Try Your Solutions Out*

The prototypes developed in the last stage and then shown to the users to obtain their feedback. This is an iterative process so it may result in a redefinition of the problem, or you may end up making further iterations, alterations, and refinements to find or rule out alternative solutions.

Stage 6: Implement – *Execute the Change*

Once you have settled on a solution it is time to turn the prototype into a finished solution and then roll it out.

Now that you have a basic understanding of the design thinking process it is time to explain how to use this process in relation to different types of work.

As with all the other T-Shaped Lawyer skills, design thinking can be used in connection with:

- internal business work, and
- to some extent, legal work, and
- client business work.

Using design thinking for legal work and internal business work.

Like the other skills, the use of the prefix *'legal'* indicates that design thinking is being used in relation to legal work or internal business work. In this situation it is commonly referred to as ***legal design.***

Legal Design has been defined as '*design deployed in the field of law to transform legal products, services, work, systems, business strategies, ecosystems and user experience.*[57]'

Legal Design is a skill is used, for example, to:

- improve presentations and other communications.
- draft more customer friendly contracts and policies.
- provide more readable opinion letters.
- enhance the customer experience of dealing with lawyers.
- re-design the organisation structure of your firm or legal department.
- improve the user experience of any products or services that you offer to clients.

One point that is worth highlighting is that typically Legal Design almost always starts with an idea, service or a product and then seeks to make it better. In other words, in practice, those using Legal Design tend to skip the first few stages of the process above and tend to start at stage 3 or 4.

How to use design thinking to do business work

Like the other skills, design thinking can, and should, be used by lawyers to do client business work. This use case is rarely discussed but, again, it is the very essence of being a T-Shaped Lawyer.

I suggest that you think about Design Thinking as one, very powerful, tool as your disposal when you are engaged in **business leadership**.

With your Businessperson Mindset you should be looking out for systemic business problems or business opportunities. In many cases that problem or opportunity can be addressed by using other skills and competencies such as problem solving or process improvement, without the need to use Design Thinking.

However, **some problems are more complex, intractable, or not obvious or easy to define. These problems are sometimes referred to as *wicked problems*[58].**

Design thinking is ideally suited to solving wicked problems as well as developing breakthrough innovations. If you understand design thinking at least to a basic level then you can identify situations when it will be an appropriate way to approach a business problem or opportunity.

You can then follow the business leadership step-by-step process[59] and simply suggest a design thinking project to your business and functional colleagues. Alternatively, you can initiate ,or even lead, such a design thinking workshop depending on your time and skill level.

Example: Contract simplification or transformation

This example illustrates a potential significant difference between applying a typical Legal Design approach compared with using the full Design Thinking process.

Legal Design is often used to simplify the wording or the look and feel of a contract. There is nothing wrong with doing that and the outcome will invariably be an improvement.

However, if you were to apply Design Thinking, you would not start with the product – in this case a contract – or assume that it is needed. Rather, you would start at Stage 1 with trying to understand the user and their needs.

Applying this approach, you may discover that, in some cases, the optimal solution is to not have a 'traditional' contract at all! Indeed, I have arrived at this conclusion in what I refer to as **'the paperless contracting' initiative.** Here we were able to eliminate the need for a written signed contract in many cases because we found alternative ways to document the essential terms with a sufficient degree of certainty. That was a breakthrough innovation, a true transformation, not just an improvement.

Example : Reimagining Compliance Training

Compliance training for corporate employees is an example of a wicked business problem. It 'ticks the box' from a legal compliance perspective. However, it is an intractable business problem because corporate employees typically do not engage with compliance training, and it rarely increases awareness or changes behaviour in any significant way. This situation is despite numerous efforts to improve training by making it more relevant, more humorous, or more visually interesting.

When I was head of global compliance several years ago, I led a design thinking workshop to tackle this wicked problem. Applying design thinking resulted in unique insights, such as those shown in the graphic below for one user group. That allowed us to re-frame the problem from trying to train employees on policies and the law to trying to help them avoid getting into trouble in situations relevant to their work.

Compliance Training Insights

USER	NEEDS	INSIGHT
Sales Employee	To know what are the most common situations where they could get into legal and financial problems in the course of their work.	• Not interested in being 'trained' on legal compliance topics. • Don't really understand why they are asked to do training – presumably it is 'for the company' • Just click through current training and don't pay attention. • Don't want to inadvertently do something that could jeapordise their job so want to know the potential pitfalls • Only want to know about things relevant to their job • Also, would like to know what to do when they face these situations – simple Do's and Don'ts

Based on those insights I developed a breakthrough approach involving a series of videos called Trouble Traps™. Unlike most compliance training, these videos are not based on legal topics. Rather they are based on typical activities and interactions, such as entertaining customers, dealing with distribution partners and interacting with vendors. 3–4-minute videos that covered the key legal and compliance issues through practical 'do's and don'ts'.

TROUBLE TRAPS®

Design Thinking may be one of the most important non-legal skills for lawyers because it helps you to see familiar problems in new ways through the eyes of your clients. In my experience, lawyers struggle to learn how to do this but, when they do, it can be a revelation.

Learning this skill is one of the best ways to overcome the insular tendency of most lawyers and it facilitates the T-Shaped Lawyer vision of looking to help clients in new ways because it requires you to put yourself in your client's shoes.

At least initially, most lawyers may not use design thinking on a regular basis. However, when you do use it, the impact can be significantly greater than any other skill that you might use more often. Over time, design thinking is a skill that lawyers may use more frequently.

As I highlighted in my first book, identifying and addressing unseen problems and opportunities for your clients is precisely what experts at Deloitte suggest is the future of work and what I would say is the ultimate embodiment of being a T-Shaped Lawyer.

3. How to develop your design thinking skills

There are many in-person and virtual courses available on design thinking. For further reading about this key skill see these references[60]. Again, it is recommended to participate in design thinking workshops whenever you get the opportunity. In fact, most progressive legal service providers have their own design thinking experts. If you work in a firm, seek them out. If you work in-house, often you can arrange for these experts to help facilitate design thinking workshops without necessarily paying for this service.

As highlighted throughout this chapter, all the T-Shaped Lawyer skills can be used for internal business work and in a few cases in relation to legal work. Indeed, most commentators in the legal industry will refer to these skills in that context, which is why the word 'legal' is added as a prefix to these skills.

There is absolutely nothing wrong with using these skills in that way. However, the important thing is for you to be able to recognise when this is the case and to understand that the same skills can be used to do client business work as explained in this chapter. By doing the latter, you can realise the T-Shaped Lawyer vision and add more value for your clients. That is why I do not use the prefix 'legal' when I describe these skills in the T-Shaped Lawyer Framework.

The next chapter will outline some key competencies that can be used to help you be a better lawyer and do better legal work. However, and this is the focus of the next chapter, they can also help you to be a different lawyer and to do client business work.

CHAPTER 4

T-SHAPED LAWYER COMPETENCIES

People often confuse competencies with skills and that is understandable. **Technical competencies** are like skills in that they help you to do specific work tasks. Examples for lawyers include drafting litigation pleadings, trademark registrations or conveyancing.

However **behavioural competencies**, such as those shown in the Framework, are different in a few ways:

- Most people will have at least some idea about behavioural competencies even if you have never studied them, whereas you need to specifically learn a skill or a technical competency to understand what it is and how to use it.
- That said, you can learn most skills or technical competencies, and be able to use them in your work, relatively quickly at least to a basic level. Behavioural competencies take much longer to learn and the impact on your work may not be as immediate. In that respect they are more like qualities.
- **Technical competencies for lawyers are only relevant to legal work, whereas behavioural competencies can also help you do internal business work and client business work**. In fact, behavioural competencies are critical to doing business work.

Because the Framework focuses on how to be a T-Shaped Lawyer to do business work, not just legal work, technical competencies are not covered in the book[61]. What is covered in the Framework, and in this chapter, are some key behavioural competencies that are the most relevant to becoming a T-Shaped Lawyer and doing business work, not just legal work. These competencies are shown below.

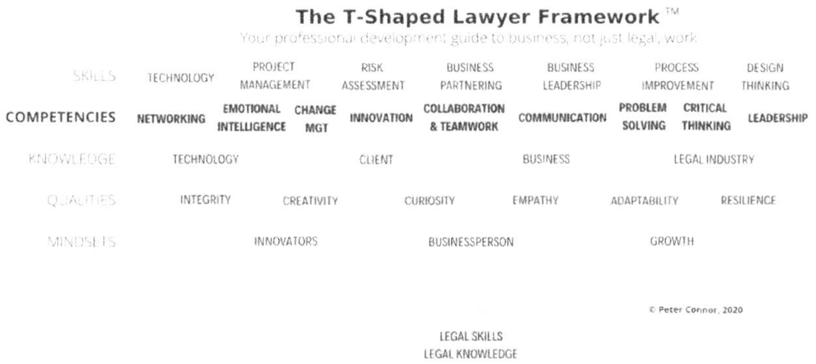

As there are entire books written on each of these competencies, my aim is not to cover them in detail. Rather, I shall focus on how these competencies are relevant to you as a corporate lawyer.

For each of the T-Shaped Lawyer competencies I will provide:

1. **a brief overview of the competency**
2. **an explanation of how to use the competency for the different types of legal and business work, and**
3. **some recommendations on how to develop the competency.**

A. Leadership

Leadership has always been important in any organisation. In times of significant change[62], leadership becomes even more critical, not only to manage that change but also to lead change or innovation within your legal department, company, or law firm.

Many lawyers mistakenly believe that leadership is only for those in leadership or management positions in a legal department, company, or law firm. However, as Donald McGannon famously said, ***'leadership is action, not a position'***.

In other words, anyone, at any stage of their career, can be a leader irrespective of whether you are in a position of authority, manage people, or not.

Leadership and management are vast topics covered in numerous courses and publications that are widely available[63]. My aim in this book is not to try to summarise those topics from a traditional perspective. Rather I will highlight some key points that are not typically covered and especially point out how you can show leadership beyond the traditional and commonly understood ways.

Let's start by establishing some leadership fundamentals and clarify some common misunderstandings.

1. What is leadership?

My favourite definition of leadership is *'the ability to influence people to willingly follow'*[64].

We all know people who are managers but who are not really leaders because they do not have this ability. Those who report to such managers may do as the manager says, but they do not always do it willingly. They do it to keep their jobs. This 'command and control' style of management is popular in some parts of the world.

Conversely, **even if you are not in a position of authority, you can be an effective leader if you develop and display this ability**. Your ability to lead does not come from your title or position. Rather it comes from your desire to make a difference and your ability to influence others to support you even if they do not report to you.

2. How to use leadership in your work

There are several different ways that every corporate lawyer can show leadership. The different types of leadership, and how you can utilise leadership competencies in these different contexts, is set out below.

i. Leadership in your legal department or your law firm ('Legal Leadership')

For every corporate lawyer the most obvious opportunity to show leadership in a work context is within your legal department or law firm. This is sometimes referred to as *Legal Leadership*[65].

Legal leadership is relevant to both:

- those in leadership positions in the legal department or firm

- and to others.

Before we explore how both these groups can show legal leadership it is helpful to understand the distinction between management and leadership.

Leadership compared with management

Steve Jobs, the founder of Apple, famously said *'Management is about persuading people to do things they do not always want to do, while leadership is about inspiring people to do things they never thought they could.'*

Simply put, leadership is about setting the direction or vision of a company, department, or firm while management is about executing that vision to turn it into reality. Leaders are more concerned with the big picture and strategic planning, while managers are more focussed on the here and now and on short term objectives.

The table below shows some further differences between leadership and management.

	Leadership	**Management**
Meaning	Influencing others to follow	Ensuring things are done right
Basis	Trust	Control
Emphasis	Inspiring people	Managing activities
Power	Influence	Position & authority

Focus	Encouraging change	Bringing stability
Strategy	Proactive	Reactive
Formulate	Vision, mission, priorities & strategies	Policies, procedures, challenges, action plans
Perspective	LT- futuristic	Short to medium term

Ideally legal departments and firms need both effective leaders and effective managers. The reason that this book focuses on leadership and not management is because:

- leadership is more important to being a T-Shaped Lawyer and doing client business work, and
- managing people and resources is more widely understood than leadership, and
- there is usually plenty of resources available for you to enhance your management competency.

With that as background, lets now explore how you can display legal leadership whether you have been appointed as a manager , leader or not.

Legal leadership by legal leaders/managers

There are many opportunities for legal leaders/managers to show leadership in discrete areas such as process, technology, and people.

That said, if you are part of the leadership team of a legal department or firm, then one area that is typically ripe for leadership is to ensure that there is a clear and aligned

statement of vision, mission, priorities, and strategic initiatives. The crucial importance of vision was explained in detail in Chapter 3 of the first book.

I do not plan to repeat that discussion again but will simply point out that *'if you create sincere and sustainable passion around a compelling vision, team members will readily follow'*[66].

When I raise the importance of vision, along with the other foundational components of a legal department or firm, with leadership teams I am often told either that we:

- *'do not think we need a vision, it sounds unnecessary', or*
- *'have a vision and that is to be the 'premier' law firm or legal department', or*
- *'just follow the corporate vision in the case of a legal department.'*

If you do not articulate a compelling vision, you should not expect the team to change much, and your role becomes more of a manager than a leader. However, if you do want the team to change and head in a different direction, such as that proposed in the first book, then vision is crucial. This type of transformative change is a special kind of change that requires a special kind of leadership as explained below.

Adaptive leadership

Leadership is, by definition, about influencing others to change. **It is crucial to understand that there are different types of challenges, different types of change and different types of**

leadership required to address these challenges and effect these changes.

One important distinction is between *technical* challenges and change, on the one hand, and *adaptive* challenges and change on the other. The table below shows some of the typical differences between the two types of challenges.

Technical challenges	**Adaptive challenges**
Easy to identify & define	Difficult to define, easy to deny
Solutions often known	No obvious solution- need to experiment
Experts can solve it	Need to involve impacted staff
Using known information	Need new ideas & approach
Small changes within org	Multiple changes beyond org
Managers can mandate	Requires changes in beliefs, attitudes, and behaviours
Often short time frame	Takes time to change
Fixes immediate problem	Provides long term outcomes
Often receptive to change	Resistance to change certain

As Ronald A. Heifetz and Marty Linsky say in their book *'Adaptive Leadership: The Heifetz Collection*[67]*'*:

'adaptive change stimulates resistance because it challenges people's habits, beliefs, and values' 'There is a proportionate relationship between risk and adaptive change: the deeper the change and the greater the amount of learning required, the more

resistance there will be and, thus, the greater the danger to those who lead. For this reason, people try to avoid the dangers by treating an adaptive challenge as if it were a technical one. This is why we see so much more routine management than leadership'. 'The single most common source of leadership failure is when people, especially those in positions of authority, treat adaptive challenges like technical problems'[68]

Despite these 'dangers' of adaptive leadership, and the fact that it involves putting yourself and your ideas 'on the line', Heifetz central thesis is that it is worthwhile and necessary. Worthwhile, because you can make the lives of others around you significantly better. **Necessary, because *'without learning new ways – changing attitudes, beliefs and behaviors – people cannot make the adaptive leap necessary to thrive in the new environment.'***

For a deeper understanding of adaptive leadership, I highly recommend reading Heifetz's books. However, the following are some of the key ideas he makes about adaptive leadership:

- It is important to identify and define the underlying adaptive challenge
- Use that to frame the key questions to identify the adaptive change required
- Allow a certain amount of pressure and discomfort for your people
- Disorienting current roles will be inevitable and desirable
- Expose conflicts and do not be in a rush to restore order
- Challenge norms and the way things have always been done
- Think politically – find partners

The subject matter of my two books perfectly illustrates this distinction between technical and adaptive challenges, change and leadership.

The primary problem, challenge or priority addressed in the books is *how can lawyers add significantly more value for their clients.*

If you treat that as a technical challenge, as most do, then it is no surprise that most of the changes suggested or implemented are technical changes such as using technology to augment the existing work done by lawyer, to enhance efficiency and reduce cost. Such changes can mostly be made by experts using known solutions, without lawyers having to change their beliefs or typically without any significant change in their behaviour or work.

But the crucial question is:

Will changes of that type address the underlying challenge? Will these changes result in adding substantially more value for the client's business?

I believe not and so do most business clients when you talk to them.

That challenge is an adaptive challenge, and it requires an adaptive change. That change, I have suggested, is to become a T-Shaped Lawyer – a businessperson who provides business advice and input, not just legal advice, and who does business work, not just legal work for the benefit of the business, not just the legal department or firm.

Adaptive leadership is required to lead a legal department or firm to make this change. How to achieve this is beyond the scope of this book but is something that I cover in my T-Shaped Team Framework™ and T-Shaped Firm Framework™.

Legal leadership for non-leaders

As mentioned above, you can be a leader in a legal department or firm even if you are not appointed as such. Those who are not appointed to be leaders are rarely asked by leaders to lead and so typically assume that they should just focus on their daily tasks and nothing else. You may never be asked by partners of firms and leaders of legal departments to do more than that.

However, one of the great ironies is that these leaders almost always[69] appreciate it if you do assume some additional responsibility and do things to help the department or firm. The reason for that is simple; they need help and cannot do it all themselves.

To put it in simple terms, start acting like the leader that you want to be. The way to do that is think as if you are a partner or a general counsel, to adopt the Businessperson Mindset and to **look for ways to make a difference in your legal department or firm.**

A useful metaphor that I use to explain the idea of making a difference is ***'moving the needle'***.

Source: https://betravingknows.com/articles/media-advertising/2019/five-ways-to-move-the-needle/ accessed November 29, 2023

Most lawyers who are not appointed as a leader focus almost exclusively on doing an excellent job in relation to each transaction or matter that they work on. If you do that then the transaction or matter may be successfully concluded, and your client and your manager may thank you. Doing this legal work well is the minimum standard that leaders expect of you as a lawyer.

However, this work typically does not improve the state of the legal department or the firm. The department or firm remains more or less the same after you have concluded that work.

Moving the needle involves doing different work, internal business work, to enhance the department or firm. After doing this type of work, the department or firm is in a better place.

Examples: Moving the needle could be:

- helping to resolve a known problem in the department or firm.
- identifying a new problem and proposing a course of action to resolve it.
- identifying an opportunity to improve the success of the department or firm.

ii. Leadership beyond the legal department or firm

Legal Leadership or leadership to benefit your department or firm is one thing and worth pursuing as explained above. However, as I explained in my first book, a T-Shaped Lawyer can and should also look for opportunities to show leadership for your clients. I refer to it as **business leadership.** I dedicate an entire chapter to this form of leadership in the first book and I encourage you to read it.[70]

Doing client business work, especially business leadership, is the very essence of being a T-Shaped Lawyer. As Heifetz states;

'to act outside the narrow confines of your job description when progress requires it lies close to the heart of leadership'[71].

3. Developing your leadership competency

You can of course take courses and do further reading on leadership. However, in my experience, the best way to enhance your leadership competency is to 'just do it' as explained above.

For those of you worried about whether you have the time to focus on leadership on top of getting through your daily tasks, it is important to highlight that:

- Leadership is not about doing everything yourself. It is about influencing a group of people to come together to work on an initiative. Those people may be within your practise group or legal department but many times it will be necessary to involve other lawyers and non-legal professionals and, sometimes, people from outside the firm or department.
- Showing leadership by, for example, moving the needle in your department or firm, is one of the best ways to help your promotion prospects as compared with just focussing on your legal skills and day job. In other words, even if it does take up additional time, it is time well spent and very rewarding for you.
- Chapter 7 of the first book provides a guide to how to manage your time commitment to business leadership initiatives.
- There are ways for in-house lawyers to manage your work to do less work that is low impact leaving you more time to do more work that moves the needle.

In summary, this section has shown the many ways that you can display leadership whether you have been appointed a leader or not. The following section of this chapter will show you the many ways you can display management capability whether you have been appointed as a manager or not.

B. Change Management

For small changes that do not impact people in any significant way you can simply make the change and move on. **However, if you are going to initiate, or be part of, any significant change that impacts people**, whether that is a change to a process, implementing a new technology solution or an organisational change, **then it is crucial to understand and utilise change management theories.**

Many significant change initiatives do not achieve their desired outcomes because of a failure to apply change management principles. It is not enough to prescribe the change and expect it to happen. Successful change involves an understanding of what must take place to make the change happen.

Example: if a legal department or firm wanted to realise the T-Shaped Lawyer vision, that involves significant change for people including:

- changes in what work lawyers do. In the case of in-house lawyers, any change in the work that they do typically has a knock-on effect on those colleagues that interact with that lawyer.
- a change to the professional development programs in a legal department or firm to help lawyers to do this different work. It also should involve a change in recruitment, performance evaluation, recognition and perhaps the organisation structure.

- changes to legal department and firm processes and technologies.
- changes to the business that follow from some of the above changes.

Change Management is therefore one of the most important competencies for lawyers to develop and use to realise the T-Shaped Lawyer vision. But it also applies to any change initiative that impacts people. **Learning how to apply change management principles maximises your chances of turning great ideas into lasting change**. It is also an essential competency for adaptive leadership as explained earlier in this book.

1. What is Change Management?

The definition of Change Management according to Prosci - one of the leading change management organisations - is '*the application of a structured process for leading the people side of change to achieve a desired outcome*'[72].

As shown in the diagram below, significant changes may impact different people – lawyers, clients and others in the legal department or firm – in various ways.

Source: https://www.prosci.com/resources/articles/definition-of-change-management accessed December 10, 2023.

Change management is typically used in conjunction with project management. '***Project management*** *focuses on the tasks required to successfully design, develop, and deliver the project from a technical perspective.* ***Change Management*** *focuses on the people impacted by any change and enables them to engage, adopt and use the change'*[73].

Change management, like project management, is also a profession. That means that there is a plethora of resources[74] available to enhance your change management competence from basic all the way to expert level. As a T-Shaped Lawyer you do not need to be an expert, but a basic level of competence is essential.

You may recall that management as a competence was raised in the discussion above to contrast it with leadership. In that context we are talking about someone, who has been appointed as a manager, managing people who report to the manager and other resources. Change management is different. **Change management is relevant to anyone, whether a manager or not, who is involved in a change that has a significant impact on people, whether in the same department or practise group or not.**

2. How to use change management in your work

Change management is a competency that you would use the same way whether you are using it for internal business work, to manage a change just within the legal department or firm, or for client business work, to manage a change that involves people outside the legal department or firm.

Just like with process improvement and project management, there are different change management methodologies you can follow.

Some well-known change management models are:

- Prosci's ADKAR[75]
- Lewin's change management model[76]
- Kotter's 8 step change model[77]
- McKinsey's 7S model[78]
- The Kubler Ross Change Curve[79]

To explain how change management works, I have selected a model devised by General Electric that I prefer to use.

Example: GE's Change Acceleration Process

This method is depicted in the graphic below.

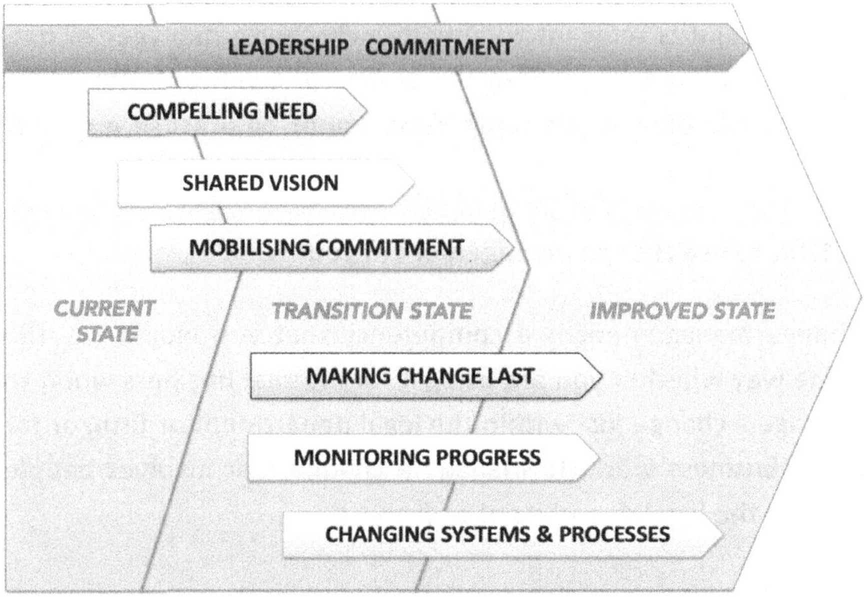

The following is a brief description of the different elements of this method which are not necessarily considered sequentially.

- **Leadership commitment**. Obtaining the buy-in of the relevant senior leadership is crucially important. If you do not secure that first, and if leadership does not actively and regularly support the change, then it will be difficult to achieve lasting change.
- **Shared compelling need.** It is not enough, as most do, to just explain the reasons for change in terms of why the change is better for the firm, legal department, or company. **It is imperative to articulate the compelling reasons for change from the perspective of every group of people who are impacted by the change.** The reason for that is simple. People

will not change unless they consider it is in their interests to change. This should be obvious and yet this crucial step is almost always overlooked.

- **Shared Future State Vision.** Another crucial step in the change management process that is often overlooked is painting a clear picture of what the future will look like for those impacted after the change. Again, the reason for this should be obvious. Who is going to change unless they have a clear idea of what their work would look like if they do change? This is precisely why I devoted my first book to articulating a clear vision of, and reasons for, the change I am advocating for lawyers to become T-Shaped Lawyers.
- **Mobilising commitment**. There are a variety of measures you need to take to implement the change including constant communication to all stakeholders and those affected by the change, the need to find some champions who will help get others 'on board' with the change, and various incentives and recognition.
- **Making change last**. It is one thing to introduce a change. It is quite another thing to make it last. You need to consider how you plan to make the change an enduring one including the next two steps.
- **Monitoring progress.** Most changes that affect people do not happen overnight. Significant changes take time, and you need to monitor the situation on a regular basis to ensure that the changes are progressing as you planned and take action if they are not.
- **Changing systems and processes.** One of the best ways to create enduring change is to change processes and systems that embed the change. Without this process and system

change, there is a risk that people will slip back into old ways of doing things.

For relatively simple changes that only impact a few people, it is not necessary to use the change management method in any formal way. It may be that you just use each of the aspects of the method as a kind of checklist to ensure that they have been considered and addressed.

3. How to enhance your change management competency

If you are only going to participate in a few change initiatives, then the explanations above may be sufficient. However, if you intend to lead change initiatives in your legal department or firm, whether as an appointed leader or otherwise, then you may wish to enhance your change management competency.

You can enhance your competency by doing further reading such as this book[80] by Kotter or by undertaking courses such as these mentioned in the end notes[81]. Also, if you have change management experts in your company or firm reach out to them. Finally, there is no better way to learn than to lead or at least participate in a change initiative.

Whatever model you choose, the point is that for any change that significantly impacts people, it is crucial to apply change management principles. Many innovation initiatives involve this sort of change as explained in the next section.

C. Innovation

Innovation is now a priority for almost every legal department, firm, and company. Without innovation it will be difficult for your department, firm, or company to keep up with the constant changes[82], let alone make significant progress.

If innovation is so important, then developing your innovation competence becomes crucial so that you can lead, or at least contribute to, innovation initiatives in your department, firm, or company. **Also, being good at innovation was rated by employers as the top 'skill' for 2025 by the World Economic Forum in their Future of Job Report[83].**

Most innovation initiatives are typically driven at a department or firm level rather than by you as an individual lawyer acting alone. There are a variety of models and approaches that firms or departments can follow for innovation. I cover these in The T-Shaped Team Framework and the T-Shaped Firm Framework. However, they are beyond the scope of this book which is focussed on individuals.

This section of the book is intended to help individual lawyers be better at innovation. An excellent place to start is by clarifying the meaning of innovation because there are a few misconceptions about it as explained below.

1. What is innovation?

There are different types of innovation such as *sustaining* and *disruptive* or transformative innovation[84]. **Most so-called**

innovation in legal departments or firm is sustaining in the sense that it makes the current situation better but does not fundamentally change or transform it.

Another way to think about this distinction is the difference between improvement or transformation as explained in the first book. Sometimes an improvement will be sufficient but, **as Google states in one of its fundamental innovation principles, you should generally aim for a 10X impact from innovation, not a 10% improvement.**

This Google innovation principle highlights one of many common misconceptions or mistakes made in relation to innovation. These include for example:

- The oft-quoted notion of the virtue of incremental 1% improvements conflate the aspiration with the execution. Of course, the implementation of any innovation will rarely be in one huge step. However, it is a mistake to set your innovation sights as low as a 1% improvement. That is hardly inspirational or aspirational enough. **As another Google innovation principle states you want to '*Think Big and Start Small*'.**
- The idea that innovation means just 'doing things differently'. In other words, any change amounts to innovation. The problem with that view is that you can end up with change for the sake of change – and I see that all too often. **Innovation involves more than just doing something different or new**, as explained below.
- The notion that innovation is all about creativity and coming up with ideas. Ideation is a crucial part of the innovation

process. However, it is only one part of that process and **ideation needs to be structured and focussed and not random as is often the case with 'idea boxes'.**

- The common approach of appointing one person or team to lead innovation within a firm or department. While it is important to have someone to drive innovation initiatives, it is critical that **everyone in a department or firm is involved in innovation and that it becomes 'just the way we work' rather than viewed as projects run by others**.

Because of these misconceptions there are a variety of definitions of innovation that are not that helpful. But here is a simple definition that I believe captures the key concept.

Innovation = Change that Adds Value

There are few key points to highlight about this definition:

Change – new ideas are important, but **ideas need to be turned into change to constitute innovation.** Change management often comes into play here.

Adding Value – the change must make a significant difference for it to constitute innovation. Not every change qualifies as innovation. The term 'adding value' is widely used but often not well understood or clearly defined. A detailed discussed of this topic, that I devote a lot of time to in my workshops, is beyond the scope of this book. However, let me make a few points:

- Value is not necessarily a financial measure.
- There are many kinds of value including emotional value and various kinds of functional value.
- In simple terms **I define value as something that is perceived as important from the perspective of the beneficiary**.

This last point is a nice segue to the next section on how to use innovation in your work because who benefits from innovation matter enormously.

2. How to use innovation in your work

When you hear people speaking about innovation in the corporate legal industry, almost always they are talking about change that adds value **to the legal department or firm**. In other words, they are referring to **internal innovation** and doing **internal business work.** A more accurate description of this might be **legal innovation**.

Using innovation for internal business work

If internal business work involves a change from the prior way of doing things and that change results in a significant added value for the legal department or firm, then it may constitute innovation.

Examples:

- A work process change that significantly reduces the amount of time required for lawyers to complete the work or, even better, means that clients can self-serve with no lawyer involvement.
- The introduction of a new system that reduces cycle time, provides greater transparency and enhanced quality control.
- Overhauling the engagement model for third party legal service providers that results in significant cost reductions.

If your legal department or firm has access to internal or external resources to drive these initiatives, then your role as a lawyer in the innovation may be limited. That said, there are various roles that you can play in innovation as explained below and your contribution may be just to identify the opportunity or suggest the solution.

Adding value for your legal department or firm is important from the perspective of the firm or department. **However, typically these internal innovations matter less (or not at all) to those that should matter most – your client.**

When you research innovation, you will see countless references to **'the customer'** as the focal point of business innovation. For example, Jeff Bezos the founder of Amazon said *' we (Amazon) innovate by starting with the customer and working backwards'.*

Starting with the customer and working backwards, is precisely how design thinking works, as explained in the last chapter. It is also how the other tools that I use in my innovation workshops are applied.

I am highlighting this as an segue to the next section on using innovation for client business work.

Using innovation for client business work

Who is the customer for a corporate lawyer?

You could say that the ultimate customer is the buyer of the products or services supplied by your client's business. In some cases, those purchasers may be your 'customer' for the purposes of innovation.

However, in a practical sense, 'your customer' for the purposes of innovation is typically the relevant business and functional executives of the client organisation. The reason for that is because you are primarily providing your services, and any products, to help them in their work.

If you work in a firm, then your 'customer' may also be the in-house legal team.

Given that the business world places the customer at the centre of innovation, I think we should do likewise. If we place 'the customer' at the centre of our idea of innovation, then our definition of innovation changes somewhat to the following:

Innovation = Change that Adds Value for your Customer

Defining innovation in this way, has many benefits:

- it shifts the focus our innovation efforts from just internal business work to client business work.
- it means that the benefits of this innovation work accrue primarily to the client and not just to the legal department or firm.
- It will be noticed, and valued, more by those clients than internal innovation. After all, your paramount change objective[85] should be to add more value for our clients.
- it personifies what it means to be a T-Shaped Lawyer and aligns your efforts to be a T-Shaped Lawyer with innovation for clients.

The key to innovating for clients is to have the Businessperson and Innovators Mindsets, to understand your clients and the work that they do, and to look beyond your immediate tasks for business problems and opportunities.

The T-Shaped Lawyer skills and competencies provide you with a range of different ways that you can innovate for your clients depending on the situation. Sometimes the situation may call for process improvement, other times a technology solution or a design thinking workshop.

Remember when you are innovating for your clients you are engaging in business leadership, and it is pertinent to recall the discussion on how to do that in Chapter 7 of the first book.

It should by now be apparent to you that, by being a T-Shaped Lawyer as proposed in the first book, you will automatically be setting yourself up to innovate in this way because it is business

work, not legal work, that helps you to innovate for not just your department or firm but for the business – your customer.

3. How to enhance your ability to innovate

As mentioned above, the key to innovation is to focus on 'your customer'. There are many different tools that can be extremely helpful here but a detailed discussion of these is beyond the scope of this book. However, in general terms the idea is for you to better understand your client so that you can help them address their challenges and achieve their priorities.

It is also important to remember that you can contribute to innovation beyond coming up with ideas. The FourSight Profiles[86] are a useful way to illustrate this point and to identify other ways that you can contribute to innovation. Consider which one of these profiles suits you best and look for ways to play that role in innovation initiatives in your company or firm.

Profile	Role	Qualities
Clarifier	Explores the situation and frames the problem/opportunity	Detail-oriented, curious, listens, avoids assumptions, questions
Ideator	Generate different possibilities	Big-picture thinker, creative, flexible
Developer	Design and plan solutions	Meticulous, pragmatic, reflective
Implementor	Put solutions into practice	Persistent, decisive, execution-focused

Your innovation competence is a function of many different things. It involves the Innovator's Mindset as explained earlier in this book. It also involves a range of other T-Shaped Lawyer skills, competencies, qualities, and knowledge such as curiosity, creativity, design thinking and general business knowledge. Also, because innovation is about change, the competencies of leadership and change management, discussed above, often come into play in innovativeness. Developing these T-Shaped Lawyer Framework components will help you to be better at innovation.

Finally, there are many free general courses and resources[87] available to enhance your innovativeness.

Innovation is rarely something done by individuals working alone. As such the next T-Shaped Lawyer competence - teamwork and collaboration - is extremely important to innovation.

D. Teamwork and Collaboration

Lawyers, especially those working in firms, typically work alone or perhaps together with other lawyers. You may interact with clients to obtain information and to provide the advice or documentation. However, most lawyers rarely work in teams with non-legal professionals and do not often look to collaborate with them.

This 'siloed' way of working may have served lawyers well in the past and may not have given rise to any issues primarily because doing just legal work can often be done in isolation. **However, if you want to be a T-Shaped Lawyer and provide business input and do business work, not just legal work, it is obvious that you need to work together with other lawyers and non-legal professionals on a more regular basis.** Collaboration with non-legal professionals lies at the very heart of the t-shaped professional concept as explained in the first book.

There is a noticeable trend in companies for employees to work in teams[88] because of the evidence in support of enhanced performance and other benefits. There is also a trend in more progressive departments and firms for lawyers to work together with non-legal professionals at least for internal business work. This is yet another reason for lawyers, especially those working in-house, to enhance their teamwork and collaboration competencies.

1.What is teamwork and collaboration and how are they different?

Teamwork is the ability to work effectively with other members of a team to achieve the desired objectives in an efficient and harmonious way. The team may be a permanent team such as a practise group in a firm or a legal department in a particular country. Alternatively, it may be a virtual team of people who do not normally work together but come together to work on a particular project and then disband afterwards.

Collaboration is like teamwork, but it is typically used to refer to situations where the people you work together with are not from the same group or organisation and, often, are non-legal professionals such as finance, HR, or IT professionals.

Teamwork often involves a more established structure with someone, the leader of the team, often a manager, in a position of authority making the key decisions. Collaboration, on the other hand, typically involves a less established structure and relies more on influence and persuasion to make decisions and produce deliverables. Whilst there is an overlap between these two competencies, they do involve some different capabilities.

2. How to use teamwork and collaboration in your work

Teamwork and collaboration for legal work is something you undoubtedly understand when and how to do. Using these competencies for internal business work requires a bit more explanation.

Using teamwork and collaboration for internal business work

As I mentioned in the first chapter of my first book, teamwork and collaboration has become increasingly popular in legal departments and firms.

Examples:

- **Within the legal department,** collaboration has been facilitated by the more widespread use of collaboration technologies[89], and sharing has been enhanced by the desire to capture and re-use knowledge data[90], and, in some cases, new agile ways of work involving more transparency into work done[91].
- **Within the same organisation**, legal departments are collaborating more with other colleagues in cross-functional teams as part of new, more agile organisational structures, and are also providing colleagues with access to contracts and information so they can self-help.
- Sharing of best practices **between those working in legal departments in different organisations** has occurred for many years, largely facilitated by in-house associations, however, in recent times, this has significantly increased in the legal operations area.
- Collaboration **between in-house departments and legal service providers** on deals, for example, has been enhanced by using collaborative virtual workspaces typically established by the service provider. Recently, some service providers are **co-creating**[92] solutions for legal departments often involving **hackathons**[93] and leveraging design thinking methodologies.

- Collaboration with universities to gain access to relatively cheap resources for your projects and at the same time providing students with valuable training opportunities.

The key point to remember when you are engaged in any internal business work is to be creative in your efforts to gain assistance from a wide range of internal or external resources. At the same time, be open to offering your time and expertise with others in the spirit of mutual collaboration and sharing.

Using teamwork and collaboration for client business work

Many of the above suggestions apply with equal force to client business work. Typically, client business work will involve you working in collaboration with others in the client organisation who are not lawyers in what are often called **cross-functional teams**. Teamwork and collaboration lie at the very heart of your business leadership activities.

3. How to enhance your teamwork and collaboration

Facilitating teamwork and collaboration should be a primary focus for all leaders of legal departments and firms. There are many things they can do for this purpose, but a detailed discussion of this topic is beyond the scope of this book. I will make just a few brief points about how individuals can enhance their team and collaboration competencies over and above the resources for further reading mentioned in the endnotes[94].

Developing most of the T-Shaped Lawyer skills, competencies, and qualities - especially communication, networking, leadership, and project management - will help you to be a better team player and collaborator. In addition to developing these components you can enhance teamwork and collaboration by:

- actively seeking out opportunities to work in a team or to collaborate with others.
- understanding your role and being reliable in playing that role and doing what you said you would do.
- at the same time being flexible and willing to go beyond your role when necessary to help not just the department or firm but also the client organisation.
- sharing your knowledge and expertise to help the team or collaborative effort be more successful.

Networking can facilitate teamwork and collaboration because it can provide you with useful knowledge and contacts to identify and take advantage of team and collaboration opportunities. A brief overview of networking is covered in the next section.

E. Networking

Networking has always been important for lawyers although not every lawyer enjoys it or does it on a regular basis. It can help you find new job opportunities and, if you work in a firm, it can help you find new clients or new work. Networking can also help you to feel more connected with a broader community and can help to enhance engagement in your work.

In broad terms, networking can provide you with contacts who may be able to help you at some point in the future. It is also one of the best ways to acquire useful information and the key areas of knowledge outlined in the T-Shaped Lawyer Framework.

Networking is imperative if you want to be a T-Shaped Lawyer. Without networking it would be very difficult to broaden your knowledge sufficiently, and to develop the relationships with work colleagues and others, that are necessary to engage in client business work.

Networking with clients may start out as an attempt to build relationships with people. **However, after a while, networking with your clients becomes simply how you engage in business partnering and identify opportunities to show business leadership.**

1. What is networking?

Networking involves building and maintaining a range of relationships with people that you meet through your work or socially. These relationships are typically of a professional nature.

However, some of your network may become friends, especially if you are in contact with them on a regular basis.

At a crude level, networking is about trading information with others. It is a virtuous cycle. **The more interesting and useful the information that you can share with others, the more they will be willing to share information with you. In that sense, developing the knowledge components of the T-Shaped Lawyer Framework greatly enhances your ability to network effectively especially with business clients.**

Networking can, of course, also be fun and fulfil a social purpose helping you to feel more connected.

There are many types of networking, as explained in more detail below. Historically, networking involved meeting people in person at work, in a social setting or at a conference. This form of networking is still important. However social media, especially LinkedIn, has provided new and very powerful ways to network.

2. **How to use networking in relation to your work**

Networking is a unique competency in the sense that you do not use it to do work. Rather it enables you to do work more effectively because it can provide you with helpful information and with contacts to help you in your work. In that sense, unlike other competencies, how you would use networking does not in general differ between the different types of work.

I will start by explaining two practical points about how to network before, in the following section, discussing how to enhance your networking.

i. When should you network?

To do networking well, especially for social media networking, you need to do it all the time, not just when you need help or information. The best social media networkers find a way to make it part of their daily routine which also doubles as a way to keep your knowledge current. Traditional networking at work also requires regular, although not necessarily daily, contact with your key legal and other colleagues.

Who should you network with?

Lawyers, especially those working in firms, tend to prefer to socialise and network with other lawyers. That make sense given that typically you have common backgrounds, experiences, interests, and work. It is important to develop connections with lawyers in, and outside, your department or firm so that you can, for example:

- seek informal legal opinions and other recommendations.
- know the best person to contact when you do need a formal legal opinion.
- informally develop your legal knowledge and skills.
- enhance your career prospects in and outside your department and firm.

- attract and retain clients in the case of lawyers working in firms.

However, a T-Shaped Lawyer should network with a diverse range of people, not just with lawyers, because you want to be a businessperson not just a lawyer.

If you work in a legal department then the following are typically important non-legal professionals to network with:

- members of the relevant business management team. That team may be the senior executives of the company if you work at corporate headquarters and have access to them through your work. Alternatively, it may be a regional, divisional or product team that you support or have the opportunity to contact regularly.
- the administrative assistants to the key management executives. Developing relationships with these assistants is often the best way to find out what is going on and, of course, to arrange meetings with these executives.
- functional peers such as Finance, HR, Marketing, and IT.
- any legal operations colleagues.

If you work in a firm, then the following are typically important non-legal professionals to network with:

- management executives of your key clients as and when appropriate.
- business development professionals in the firm.

- any experts in technology, process improvement, and project management in the firm.

3. How to enhance your networking

Some people find it easy to network and enjoy doing it on a regular basis. Others struggle with networking and do it reluctantly. Below are some general tips for enhancing your networking competency.

Networking typically works best if you can develop a personal relationship not just a purely professional relationship. That does not mean that you must become friends and socialise with every contact after work. However, it helps if you are willing to share some personal information with those in your network – keep it casual and just have a conversation. If you do that, it tends to encourage the other person to reciprocate, leading to greater trust and a deeper relationship.

Ironically, although the primary objective in networking is to have a range of contacts who can help you, the most effective way to network is to focus on how you can help those in your network. There are various ways to help those in your network ranging from a phone call to a social media post on a topic of interest. The more you are seen as giving to others, the more others will want to give to you. The power of giving is highlighted in the book *"Give and Take: Why Helping Others Drives our Success*[95]*"* by Professor Adam Grant.

One of the key challenges with networking is how to balance the time you spend networking with the multitude of other professional and personal things you need to do. The best way to manage your time, and to enhance your networking effectiveness, is to have a plan such as the one below.

State your objectives: What are you trying to achieve?	**Identify your existing networks.**
Outline who to connect with and when and how you will do so	**Specify how you will expand and maintain your relationships**
Allocate appropriate amounts of time	**Update the plan regularly**

While the above comments apply to both traditional networking and virtual networking, these forms of networking are so different that it is helpful to discuss them separately.

Traditional in-person networking

In-person networking is a very effective way to network because it is easier to build a relationship with someone face-to-face than it is virtually. With remote working now more prevalent, in-person networking opportunities may be more limited. However, when you can create these opportunities at, and beyond, the office they can be very impactful.

At the office, every interaction with a work colleague, whether you bump into someone in the office or are in a meeting or on a call, is a chance to network. So be ready to use these interactions for that purpose and not just to discuss the immediate topic at hand. That means:

- Be personable and, at the beginning of the chat, meeting, or call, if it is appropriate in your culture and the situation, **discuss non-work-related topics especially if they are about your colleague/s and not just about you**.
- Adjust the communication to the seniority of the colleague. For example, be more succinct and strategic with a senior executive that you barely know.
- Try to share something new and interesting with the colleague/s.
- Ask a colleague what their current challenges and priorities are.
- If appropriate and time permits, briefly update the colleague on what the department/firm is doing especially if it relates to one of these challenges or priorities.
- Listen for any new or interesting information from your colleague/s.

- Engage in business partnering by providing business input and/or business advice where appropriate in addition to any legal advice.
- Try to create more interactions with the colleagues with whom you want to develop relationships. Examples of such interactions include a quick chat in the hallway or lunchroom, a coffee catch up, a one-on-one meeting, attending their staff meetings, or a drink or meal after work.

The comments above apply equally to people who you do not work with, although the opportunities for spontaneous interactions may be more limited. On the other hand, there are also other ways to interact with such people.

Beyond the office there are various opportunities to network with other lawyers in person including:

- various professional societies and associations such as your local law society
- inhouse groups like the Association of Corporate Counsel (ACC), European Corporate Lawyers Association (ECLA), Corporate Legal Operations Consortium (CLOC) and the various national members of In-house Counsel Worldwide
- lawyer communities such as Inhouse Connect[96], Inhouse Community[97] and InView[98]
- conferences and networking events put on by firms or other organisations
- industry networks relevant to your clients industry
- create your own network, community, or cohort as some have done.

Whereas in the past there were only a few limited options for networking, now the challenge is choosing which communities and events you want to participate in. While social considerations will no doubt be important, be mindful that some communities do not encourage diversity of thought or opportunities and you may end up hearing the same thing from the same people over and over again.

Virtual or remote networking

The increase in work-from-home arrangements does mean that the opportunities for in-person networking with work colleagues are typically more limited than they were in the past. However virtual networking does allow you to continue to network with those in your immediate geographic area and, importantly, also with those further away that you might have had difficulty networking with before.

Email, instant messaging, and video conference calls all provide convenient ways to make, and stay in touch with, key contacts. However, it is social media that provides the opportunity to supercharge your networking and, at the same time, help you to expand your knowledge.

Social media networking

There are various social media platforms used for business purposes such as LinkedIn, Instagram, Twitter(X), and Facebook. I favour LinkedIn because it allows you to:

- sign up easily for free[99]

- position yourself to the outside world through your profile and your postings.
- follow anyone anywhere in the world.
- expand your network by connecting with someone more easily than it would be through other means.
- enhance your knowledge and be informed of the latest thinking of thought leaders.
- share your thoughts by posting or commenting on posts by others.
- over time, build a personal brand as people get to know you and the quality of your contributions on the platform.
- send a private message to anyone your connections that is more likely to be read than an email.
- identify, and be sought out for, job opportunities.

It is important to decide how you want to interact on the platform. There are those that focus on quantity of interactions whereas others prefer to focus on quality. There are many resources available to help you make the most of LinkedIn such as those mentioned in the reference section of this book[100].

Communication is obviously key to interacting well with others, to relationships and, therefore, to networking. The next section will provide some guidance on how to enhance your communication competency.

F. Communication

Communication is one of the most critical competencies for your personal and professional life. You can have the best ideas and thoughts but, if you cannot convey those in a way that your audience understands, the value of your contributions diminish significantly. Worse still, if you are a poor communicator, then you can damage your reputation, relationships, and your career.

In some respects, lawyers are generally better than non-legal professional in communicating effectively. Lawyers, because of training and work, can typically write well and provide clear verbal opinions. However, some lawyers are not as effective at, for example, listening, doing a presentation, or writing an opinion letter in simple, non-legalese form, preferred by clients.

The topic of communication is vast and there are numerous resources available to help you understand and enhance your communication competency. This section of the book will simply highlight a few points about communication of relevance to lawyers and provide some references for further reading.

1. What is communication?

When most people think about communication, they think about the one-way process of delivering information whether in written, verbal, or non-verbal means. **However, it is important to remember that communication is a two-way process that involves delivering and receiving information.**

Communication is the process of understanding and sharing meaning. That means communication is active and involves conveying and perceiving thoughts, feelings, ideas, or insights. It also means that listening is as important to communicating effectively as what you say, write or do.

2. How to use communication in your work

There are a multitude of different ways that you will communicate with lawyers and other professionals during legal, internal business and client business work. The type of work does not necessarily influence how you communicate, but who you are communicating with is crucial.

The key point is that when communicating with business executives or other non-legal professionals it is imperative to be as succinct as possible, use simple, easy-to-understand language and minimise 'legalese'. This and some other suggestions for how to enhance your communication skills are mentioned below.

For legal, internal business and client business work it is necessary to be effective at many different types of communication. For each type of communication, slightly different considerations apply such as:

- **In a one-on-one discussion,** you have a bit more latitude for how you communicate, but it is still important to listen carefully to what the other person is saying. Use the opportunity to clarify anything that is not clear and keep your comments short and to the point. Generally make the conversation about them, not about you unless you have been invited to focus on you.

- **In an email or written memo,** use clear and simple language, and avoid lengthy legal analysis. If such analysis must be included, have it at the end after an executive summary with specific recommendations about what to do or not do.
- **In a formal meeting with more than one person**, listen to the discussion even it is not about legal issues (this is your opportunity to learn not only key knowledge but also observe how others communicate). Try not to dominate the meeting but equally try not to sit there and say nothing. If you adopt the Businessperson Mindset, this is generally a prime opportunity to offer business input and advice and to look out for business leadership opportunities.
- **In a presentation to multiple people,** know your audience and target your message to that audience. Have a clear structure to your presentation with a strong compelling opening. Engage your audience as much as possible. Use slides sparingly, maximise graphics, minimise words and NEVER read what is on the slide. Prepare well. Speak clearly and mix up your speed, tone, and volume for greater impact. Be yourself, it comes across as more authentic. Check out the logistics beforehand - you do not want a technical glitch to ruin your presentation.

These are just a few tips and below are some further recommendations for how to communicate better.

3. How to enhance your communication competency

There are countless general communication courses, books and publications and some references to some of these are included below. I will highlight just a few suggestions below for improving communication that are of particular relevance to most lawyers:

- **listening.** Not all lawyers are good at listening to others, often because they are keen to speak themselves. Being a good listener and showing others that you are listening are critical aspects of good communication. To better understand the different types of listening, to assess your listening competence and for lots of useful advice on how to be a better listener, check out these resources[101] in the notes.
- **brevity.** We all know lawyers who are very verbose in their written or oral communications. At best, it is painful for those on the receiving end. At worst, the recipient loses interest, fails to listen, and does not fully understand what is being said. Making your messages more succinct is an excellent way to enhance your communications.
- **simplification**. Lawyers are often tasked with explaining to others complex matters about legal and other topics. The best communicators can do that by simplifying the message, making it easier for the other person to understand.
- **legalese**. All too often some lawyers tend to speak and write using legal terminology. That makes it difficult, if not impossible, for the recipients, especially business executives, to understand. Corporate lawyers should minimise, if not eliminate, 'legal speak' and use 'business speak' - the common terminology used by the business – as much as possible.
- **adaptability**. Some lawyers tend to communicate, whether that be orally or in writing, in one standard way irrespective of

whether they are communicating with the CEO or a junior lawyer. It is critical to adapt the message and the way in which it is communicated to the recipient and the situation. Those in senior positions generally do not want to hear about the tactical day-to-day issues and concerns unless they are symptomatic of some underlying problem that has a business impact. Also try to align what you want to say to these people with themes that are important to them.

It would be a huge undertaking to set about trying to improve all aspects of your communication all at once. Instead, it is suggested that you ascertain, through feedback and assessment, which aspects of your communication are less developed and any that are giving rise to problems for you. Focus on enhancing these aspects first and in a staged fashion. You should be able to find numerous resources to help you enhance your communications competency. I have included in the reference section of this book[102] some additional resources that you may find useful.

G. Problem Solving and Decision Making

As explained in the first book, the primary reason to become a T-Shaped Lawyer is so that you can do different kinds of work that add more value for your clients. **The key to adding value, according to the future of work experts at Deloitte, is '*to identify and address unseen problems and opportunities*'[103]. To do that sort of work, problem solving obviously becomes a critical competence for you to develop.**

You will almost certainly have developed some level of competence in problem solving through your legal training and work. However, typically that capability is developed subconsciously without any formal training or thought given to the process of problem solving.

The aim of this section of the book is to serve as a brief introduction to the competence of problem solving and how it can be used by lawyers not just to solve legal problems but also business problems. We will also in this section briefly cover decision making which is part of problem solving but also represents a stand-alone competence.

1. What is problem solving?

A problem is an obstacle or barrier that prevents the achievement of a goal or desired outcome. Problem solving is the ability to remove or overcome any barrier so that the goal can be achieved.

Problems come in all shapes and sizes. The following are a few different types of problems.

Legal problems v business problems

A legal problem typically involves a situation where a client's proposed course of action might give rise to a legal risk or liability. Lawyers are very adept at solving such problems by advising how the client can adapt their actions to achieve their objective with less risk or potential liability.

However, companies rarely have just legal problems. Rather they have business problems and legal issues may be more, or less, relevant depending on the situation. If you think about it from that perspective, as a T-Shaped Lawyer would, then it is easier to see how you can, and should, help your clients to solve not just any legal problem but broader business problems.

As Harvard Law School Professor David Wilkins puts it[104] increasingly *'neither the contours of the problem nor the possible array of solutions is strictly "legal" or fully understood by either the client or the lawyer. Instead, lawyers work collaboratively with a broad range of professionals to help clients refine their understanding of the problem and the potential array of solutions in ways that promote the client's ability to continue to make good decisions moving forward.'*

Unseen problems

Unseen problems are situations where the barrier to the business of your client is not apparent or has not appeared yet but is likely to at some point in the future.

Example: your client's business may not be running as smoothly as it could, but no-one can see that this is because there is a lack of resource or process.

Example: there is an impending regulatory change which you can foresee is going to adversely impact your client's business.

Lawyers have an advantage in identifying unseen or future problems because we are experienced at anticipating future consequences.

Wicked problems

Wicked problems are intractable problems where it is extremely difficult to understand what the problem is and how to solve it effectively.

Example: as mentioned previously, compliance training for corporate employees is an example of a wicked problem that has not been solved. There have been numerous attempts over the years to make it more interesting, fun, and relevant. However, everyone who works in company knows that most employees do not engage with it and therefore it does not achieve one of its objectives of raising awareness in any significant way.

2. **How to use problem solving in your work**

Because most lawyers are familiar with problem solving in connection with our legal work and not in relation to client business work, I shall focus on the latter in this explanation.

However, the process below applies equally to legal work and internal business work.

Lawyers will invariably be contacted by clients for help in solving a problem with a legal dimension. How can you help in solving a business problem?

As explained in the first book, there are numerous opportunities for lawyers to provide business input in every interaction with clients and to do client business work especially in areas adjacent to your legal work. The more you provide that input, the more you do that work, the more clients will proactively come to you, as a business partner or trusted advisor, to obtain your views on business problems and decisions. Also, the more you do this and the more you adopt the Businessperson Mindset, the more you will identify business problems without the need for someone to raise these with you.

Although you may not think of it this way, you follow a process to solve legal problems.

Example: you identify and categorise the problem, you gather relevant facts, review relevant documents, question relevant people, analyse the situation and arrive at a conclusion.

This process, and your experience, can also be applied to solve business problems especially if you combine it with business knowledge and other relevant T-Shaped Lawyer Framework capabilities.

Simple business problems, like simple legal problems, may be solved quickly based on intuition, common sense, or experience. More complex or unfamiliar problems will likely require a more structured approach to reach a solution.

An approach for solving more complex problems typically involves the following stages:

i. Problem identification

This first stage involves identifying if there is a problem or not. Sometimes what appears to be a problem may be simply a misunderstanding about a situation or have some other explanation.

It often helps, in this first stage, to state the goal and the barrier that is the perceived obstacle to achievement of the goal. Ultimately, the outcome of this stage should be a working definition of the problem sufficient to explain it to others.

ii. Problem definition

Problem definition is a critical stage of the problem-solving process that involves fact finding and a careful consideration of the situation. Here it is important to carefully consider:

- Is the stated goal and the stated barrier accurate?
- Is there one problem or more than one problem?
- Is the perceived problem merely a symptom of another underlying problem?

Example: the problem may be perceived initially as employees not doing their job properly thereby causing problems for customers. However, on closer examination, the real cause of that situation may be inadequate training, flawed process, or a lack of resources.

There are a variety of tools available to you to help determine the real problem when there is some complexity including the following:

- The Five Whys[105]
- Root Cause analysis[106]
- CATWOE analysis[107]
- Affinity diagrams[108]
- Cause and Effect or Fishbone diagram[109]
- Process improvement methodologies
- Design Thinking for wicked problems

As a lawyer you will typically have some skills and experience from your legal work to help determine whether there is an underlying problem. However, if you do not have a businessperson mindset, and you are too busy to think about it, you may miss that opportunity in your rush to get to the next task.

It is important in this stage to resists the urge to come up with a solution. Instead, just focus on defining the problem appropriately. Solutions are the focus of the next stage.

iii. Generating possible solutions

This stage involves generating a range of possible courses of action to solve the problem but not attempting to evaluate these possible solutions.

There are a variety of techniques that can be used in this stage. The most popular technique is brainstorming[110]. For this to work well it is important to have small group of relevant stakeholders with diverse experiences and perspectives to develop possible solutions.

iv. Making a decision

This stage involves a careful evaluation of the different courses of action identified in the prior stage and then selecting the optimal solution for implementation. Below is a more detailed discussion about decision making.

v. Implementation

Implementation means executing the chosen solution. During implementation, more problems may arise especially if identification or structuring of the original problem was not carried out properly.

Implementation of the course of action may be a simple case of assigning it to someone to go and get it done. However, if implementation of the preferred solution is complicated and requires multiple people to work together over time, then it may be beneficial to utilise project management to maximise the chances of providing the solution on time and within budget. Change management may also be required for solutions that significantly impact people. Depending on the solution, other skills, such as process improvement and technology development or acquisition may be involved.

An I-shaped lawyer typically is only involved in this final stage of problem solving by, for example, being asked by their clients to commence legal proceedings to try to resolve a problem or to draft a contract to finalise an agreed resolution to a problem.

By contrast, a T-Shaped Lawyer would move up the value chain and regularly be involved at earlier stages of the process, ideally right from the beginning in identifying the problem. This amounts to business leadership and how to do that is explained in the first book.

As previously mentioned, identifying, and addressing business problems and opportunities can be viewed as the best way to add value for your clients and as the future of work for all lawyers. **Does the approach outlined above for problems apply equally to opportunities?**

How to identify and address opportunities

A business opportunity is an initiative or change that progresses your organisation towards its goals but, unlike a problem, does not necessarily have a barrier.

Examples: Business opportunities may be significant like a new product, service, or line of business. Alternatively, the opportunity may be less earth shattering like a reduction in business risk, increase in speed or routes to market, or a chance to reduce or better align resources for more impact.

Like problems, some opportunities may be easy to identify and to implement without the need to go through a formal step-by-step process. However, more complex opportunities, like more complex problems, will benefit from a more structured approach. **In these cases, the approach outlined above for problem solving could be used to identify and exploit opportunities.**

Unlike problems, lawyers typically have less experience at identifying and exploiting opportunities. The exception to this would be at the final implementation stage where lawyers are often called in to 'cross the T's and dot the I's'. The aim of a T-Shaped Lawyer is to move up the value chain and get involved earlier in the process, ideally right at the beginning with opportunity identification. That is business leadership and how to do that is explained in detail in the first book.

Decision Making

1. What is decision making and how does it relate to problem solving?

Decision making is choosing between two or more possible courses of action. That might arise in the absence of any specific problem. However, decision making, as outlined above, may be the penultimate stage of problem solving.

Lawyers often perceive decision making as something that they are either not very good at or that it is something they should not get involved in because they are only meant to advise not decide.

2. How to use decision making in your work

When it comes to client business work then it is true that lawyers typically do not have to make business decisions for their clients. Indeed, I refer to this as the 'safety net' for lawyers engaging in business partnering. By that I mean you can offer business advice safe in the knowledge that you will rarely, if ever, be held responsible for the business decision.

However, as a lawyer you do:

- **need to make decisions about your work, your professional development and, if you are a leader, about internal business work that impacts your legal department or firm, and**
- **want to provide clients with support for the business decisions that they need to make. Clients typically ask, or want to know, '*so what do you think I should do*?' If you do not provide that recommendation then, not only do you disappoint your clients, but you miss out on another opportunity to add value.**

So, even if it is not your responsibility to make business decisions, if you want to be a T-Shaped Lawyer and to provide business advice to help your clients make optimal business decisions, then it helps for you to understand and be competent at decision making.

How to get involved in supporting business decisions may be a challenge, at least initially, for many lawyers. **However, the approach for how to get involved in business problem solving, suggested above, applies equally to decision support.**

The starting point for you to provide decision support to your clients is to have the Businessperson Mindset and start consciously thinking about what decisions do my clients make – something most lawyers rarely do - and how can you support them.

There are various ways to provide decision support to clients and a lot of this is covered in the business partnering section of the first book. However below are some of the suggestions made in that book:

- provide useful and relevant information to the decision makers.
- clarify the business objectives.
- 'join the dots' - connecting clients with other relevant people, cases, or policies.
- do risk assessment properly, as explained earlier.
- make recommendations- do not just say *'on the one hand and on the other hand'*.

To support your clients in their decision making you really need to understand how decisions are made. The following briefly explains the decision-making process.

In general, decisions can be made based on intuition or reasoning, or a combination of the two.

i. Intuition is often referred to as your 'gut feeling' or instinctive reaction. Although it sounds a bit mystical, intuition is a combination of your past experiences and your personal values. It is worth taking your intuition into account because it reflects your learning in life. However, intuition may be based more on perception than reality which may not be entirely accurate. It is worth evaluating your intuition and try to work out why you feel that way and whether that feeling is justified.

ii. Reasoning is using facts and figures, rather than emotions and feelings, to go through a process to arrive at a logical decision. You might go through that process quickly in your head or you might take time at each step and involve others in the process.

Which approach is best for business decision making?

The approach taken to each decision should vary depending on the decision to be made.

As Jeff Bezos, the founder of Amazon, said in a letter to shareholders a few years ago:

'Some decisions are consequential and irreversible or nearly irreversible – one-way doors – and these decisions must be made

methodically, carefully, slowly, with great deliberation and consultation. If you walk through and don't like what you see on the other side, you can't get back to where you were before. We can call these Type 1 decisions.

But most decisions aren't like that – they are changeable, reversible – they're two-way doors. If you've made a suboptimal Type 2 decision, you don't have to live with the consequences for that long. You can reopen the door and go back through. Type 2 decisions can and should be made quickly by high judgment individuals or small group'.

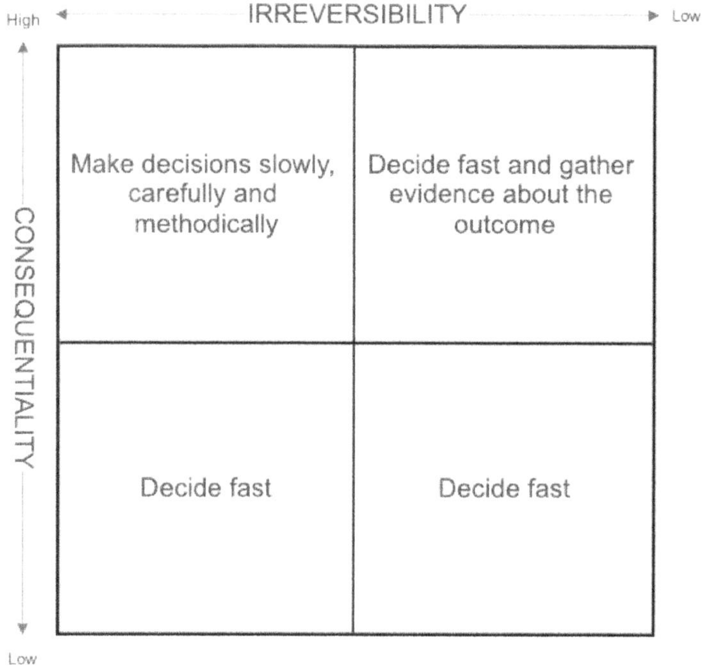

Then, in a later letter to shareholders, Bezos said:

'You have to somehow make high-quality, high-velocity decisions. Easy for start-ups and very challenging for large organizations. Speed matters in business – plus a high-velocity decision making environment is more fun too. We don't know all the answers, but here are some thoughts.

- *First, never use a one-size-fits-all decision-making process[...]*
- *Second, most decisions should probably be made with somewhere around 70% of the information you wish you had. If you wait for 90%, in most cases, you're probably being slow. Plus, either way, you need to be good at quickly recognizing and correcting bad decisions. If you're good at course correcting, being wrong may be less costly than you think, whereas being slow is going to be expensive for sure.*
- *Third, use the phrase "disagree and commit." This phrase will save a lot of time. If you have conviction on a particular direction even though there's no consensus, it's helpful to say, "Look, I know we disagree on this, but will you gamble with me on it? Disagree and commit?" By the time you're at this point, no one can know the answer for sure, and you'll probably get a quick yes.*
- *Fourth, recognize true misalignment issues early and escalate them immediately. Sometimes teams have different objectives and fundamentally different views. They are not aligned. No amount of discussion, no number of meetings will resolve that deep misalignment. Without escalation, the default dispute resolution mechanism for this scenario is exhaustion'.*

It is worth pointing out that this is not necessarily how decisions are made in your organisation. However, to the extent that you can help your clients to adopt these suggestions, it is likely to lead to optimal high quality, high velocity decision making.

Intuition may be an acceptable basis for a decision if it needs to be made quickly, you have had a lot of experience with similar situations and you do a quick sanity check based on reasoning.

But for more complicated decisions, especially those with more serious consequences and with a higher degree of irreversibility, it is important to follow a process of reasoning ideally involving others in the process[111].

There are many different methodologies[112] that can be used for decision making based on reason including a decision tree or a decision matrix[113]. **However below is a simple reason-based process that you could use for many decisions:**

> **i. Clarify objectives**. Time spent clarifying what your clients are trying to achieve can very often lead to some surprises and, of course, will frame the following decision-making stages in a very different way. Lawyers are often good at questioning, listening, and clarifying. This will help you to contribute, if not drive, this stage.
>
> **ii. Set a timescale and determine who needs to be involved in, and make, the decision**. Refer to the above comments and determine whether this is a decision that should be made quickly or not. Also determine who needs to be involved in the decision and who should make the decision. Here you need to consider any relevant signature authority policies or

processes. Also models like RACI[114] and DACI[115] are useful and may be required by some organisations. Lawyers are usually good at understanding, and explaining to others, who should make the decision and what their role is in assisting (but usually not making) the decision.

iii. **Identify possible options.** Next step is to identify, and preferably list, a range of different alternative courses of action to achieve that objective. Brainstorming and other idea generating methodologies can be used in this stage if necessary. Creativity can be very useful as well as experience with design thinking.

iv. **Information gathering.** Collect the relevant facts and any data to the extent that this exists. Check that the data is current and accurate otherwise the decision may be based on a false premise. Your skills, experience and training as a lawyer should allow you to make a significant contribution at this stage.

v. **Assess the risks.** As explained in the risk assessment discussion earlier in the book, as a T-Shaped Lawyer, you should be able to lead and contribute significantly to this step in the process. Remember to consider all risks not just legal risks.

vi. **Assess the opportunity.** Lawyers are typically less experienced at this stage of the process although the techniques involved are not dissimilar to risk assessment. It is critical to assess the potential rewards and benefits with each course of action. Consider the extent to which the opportunity might solve a problem as well as other factors such as the likelihood and potential impact of any benefits.

vii. Weigh pros and cons. Comparing the risk with the potential reward will be crucial to the decision. However, many other factors may also come into play such as the cost and resources required to implement the decision, the timing, and the impact on people, society, and the environment[116]. This stage of the process involves weighing all factors. This can be done informally in the case of relatively simple and obvious decisions. More complex decisions may require a more formal approach involving weighted balance sheet spreadsheets or some other tool such as a pre-mortem[117]. At this stage it is also sometimes helpful to consider the intuitive approach as a kind of check against the reasoned analysis.

viii. Make the decision. There are various types of decisions that could be made including for example, no action, run a pilot and proceed with a course of action but later. In the case of important decisions, where the consequences are high or it would be difficult to reverse the decision, it is good practice to document the decision and the rationale for the decision.

As you can see from the above, as a lawyer you can contribute greatly to many, if not all, stages of decision making based on your training and experience as a lawyer. Your ability to contribute will be even greater as you develop the T-Shaped Lawyer Framework capabilities.

3. How to develop your problem solving and decision making

The best way to develop these competencies is to refer to the guidance above to regularly and consciously practice using problem solving and decision making in your work. It is also possible as part of your legal team to do case studies simulations to practice these competencies.

There are also many different resources available for you to develop these competencies including these books[118] referenced in the notes.

One aspect of developing these competencies is for you to understand the factors that can assist or obstruct optimal decision making and problem solving.

Sound judgement is, understandably, a highly rated quality. Judgement is the ability to make considered and effective decisions, come to sensible solutions to problems, and form objective opinions. I chose not to include judgement as a stand-alone quality in the T-Shaped Lawyer Framework because, in relation to your work, it almost always arises as part of other skills and competencies such as business partnering, problem solving or decision making.

Good judgement is crucial to optimal decision marking, whether on a stand-alone basis or as part of problem solving. However, there are a variety of factors that can get in the way of good judgement, and therefore optimal decision making, such as:

- insufficient or inaccurate information
- biases
- preferences
- vested interests.

You may not be able to control the judgement of others but being mindful of the possible existence of these factors and guiding your clients through the decision-making process will help.

The best way to minimise any adverse impact of these factors on your own judgement is to be self-aware of your own personal biases[119] and preferences and to be able to think critically.

Critical thinking is a key T-Shaped Lawyer Framework competency and the subject of the next section of the book.

H. Critical Thinking

Critical thinking is rated by most employers and the World Economic Forum as one of the top competencies for all workers now and into the future. Importantly, it is also one that is somewhat immune from the advance of AI, at least for now.

Despite the growing importance of, and need for, critical thinking, it is often said that critical thinking is in decline. For example, Paul Hurd said, in his assessment of the general current state of critical thinking today, "*too many facts, too little conceptualizing, too much memorizing, and too little thinking*[120]". **Left to itself, thinking tends to become biased, distorted, partial, uninformed, or downright prejudicial. The result is suboptimal judgements, decision making, and problem solving.**

The following section of the book will briefly explain critical thinking and how to maintain and enhance your critical thinking.

1. What is critical thinking?

Critical thinking is the ability to question, analyse, interpret, evaluate, and make a judgement about what you read, hear, say, or write. It involves thinking about your thinking (and that of others) using standards such as clarity, accuracy, relevance, precision, logic, and significance. The term *critical* comes from the Greek word *kritikos* meaning "able to judge or discern". Critical thinking done well allows you to make sound judgements, provide constructive opinions and make optimal decisions based on reliable information.

A helpful way to understand critical thinking is to describe someone who thinks critically. A critical thinker is a person who:

▪ is inquisitive and curious	▪ questions everything, including existing assumptions, social norms, and traditions	▪ looks beyond what may appear as obvious
▪ carefully examines facts, information, and ideas	▪ is perceptive and able to make connections between different ideas	▪ uses evidence to support claims
▪ uses logic and reason in their arguments	▪ avoids making assumptions	▪ recognises (and avoids) logical fallacies
▪ is aware of their own cognitive biases and those of others	▪ is reflective and aware of their own thought processes	▪ can identify inconsistencies and errors in reasoning
▪ is open-minded and considers different perspectives	▪ thinks in a systematic way considering all elements in their wider	▪ checks their thinking for clarity, accuracy, precision, relevance, depth, breadth, significance,

	context	logic, and fairness
▪ arrives at well-reasoned conclusions		

2. How to use critical thinking in your work

Being able to think critically helps you in all types of work to:

- be conscious of, and manage, your emotions, biases, and preferences.
- assess the barrage of news, information, claims, recommendations.
- formulate your own opinions.
- make informed and reasoned decisions and judgements.

Critical thinking really forms the basis for all your legal and business work. It is also crucial in your personal and career development as well as your personal life.

3. How to develop your critical thinking

Because critical thinking is such a vast topic, I am not even going to attempt to summarise it in this book. Rather I will refer you to some resources[121] that will help you better understand and develop your critical thinking. For this book, I will highlight just a few key points to consider about critical thinking and its relevance to you and your work as a lawyer:

- As a lawyer you no doubt have developed a level of competence in critical thinking during your studies and your work. It may not have been taught to you as such but learning to 'think like a lawyer' is mostly about critical thinking.
- Often, critical thinking goes from something that you do very consciously and regularly in your studies to something that is done on a subconscious basis in your work. The potential danger is that you become worse at critical thinking unless you consciously work on maintaining and developing it as part of your professional development.
- The risk of not applying critical thinking, or not doing it well, is particularly acute when you become very busy and focussed on task completion.
- You can be capable of critical thinking, but if you do not apply it consistently, biases or emotions can emerge and interfere with your thinking.
- Typically, the more your progress in your career, especially as an in-house lawyer, it is this ability to think critically, rather than any legal knowledge, that matters more.
- Not all your clients will have this same training or experience in critical thinking. That gives you an advantage and an opportunity to add value by using critical thinking to counsel your clients and to help them arrive at better decisions and solutions to problems.
- Critical thinking is something that needs regular practice and deliberate application.

In conclusion, critical thinking may be the most fundamental and all-important competency of all. Critical thinking was key to me formulating the T-Shaped Lawyer vision, the various T-Shaped

Frameworks, and in writing the books. It should be something you use to assess my views and form your own conclusions.

I. Emotional Intelligence

Most lawyers have high cognitive and analytical intelligence. A high Intelligence Quotient (IQ) helps to obtain the marks to gain entry to law school and to do well in your studies and in your traditional legal work. However, we all know people with high IQs who do not necessarily do so well in their professional and personal life. Quite often the reason for that is because they have relatively low emotional intelligence as measured by your Emotional Quotient or EQ.

According to Daniel Goleman and many other experts, it is at least as important to be emotionally and socially intelligent as it is to be cognitively and analytically intelligent. See, for example, *Emotional Intelligence: Why It Can Matter More Than IQ*[122] and the discussion below on why it is so important.

Despite the importance of emotional intelligence, few lawyers fully understand what it means, how to use it in their work and how to enhance this crucial competency.

Let's start by clarifying what emotional intelligence means.

1. What is emotional intelligence?

Emotional intelligence has been defined as *'a set of emotional and social capabilities that influence the way we perceive and express ourselves, develop and maintain social relationships, cope with challenges and use emotional information in an effective and meaningful way'.*

According to Daniel Goleman[123], emotional intelligence has four main components as shown and explained below.

Emotional Intelligence Domains and Competencies

Self-awareness	Self-management	Social awareness	Relationship management
Emotional self-awareness	Emotional self-control	Empathy	Influence
	Adaptability	Organizational awareness	Coach and mentor
	Achievement orientation		Conflict management
	Positive outlook		Teamwork
			Inspirational leadership

Source: More Than Sound, LLC, 2017

The first two relate to you personally:

- **Self-awareness.** Unlike in Chapter 1 of this book when we were discussing the importance of you being generally self-aware, here we are specifically talking about emotional self-awareness. This means the ability to identify and understand your own emotions and the impact you have on others.

- **Self-management.** This involves the ability to manage your emotions and behaviours. It is about having the self-control to keep disruptive emotions and impulses under control and not behave in a negative way.

The second two relate to you and other people:

- **Social awareness.** This involves the ability to identify and understand the emotions of others. Primarily it requires empathy but also organisational awareness.
- **Relationship management.** Here we are talking about the ability to maintain healthy relationships by managing the emotions of others through influence, conflict management and teamwork.

As you can tell from the above description, emotional intelligence (EQ) is different to IQ.

IQ is focussed on your intellectual, analytical, logical, and rational abilities. It measures how readily you learn new things, recall information, engage in reasoning, manipulate numbers, think abstractly and analytically, and solve problems using prior knowledge.

Another difference is that IQ is relatively static and difficult to change, whereas experts confirm that you can enhance your emotional intelligence as I explain further below.

2. How to use emotional intelligence in your work

Understanding and managing our emotions, and the emotions of others, helps us to be more successful in both our personal and professional lives. That is particularly true when emotions run high. Emotions often precede thought and they change the way the brain functions, diminishing cognitive abilities, decision-making, and even interpersonal skills.

At a personal level, emotional intelligence can help you to improve personal relationships and manage your emotions so that they do not adversely impact your thinking and behaviour. In short it can help you to be happier and more successful in the sense of achieving your personal and professional goals.

In a work context, emotional intelligence can also help you to resolve conflicts and understand what is behind a decision that might otherwise seem illogical. Managing emotions is especially important in situations when you are under pressure. Lawyers are often working under pressures such as:

- meeting tight deadlines
- dealing with challenging clients or colleagues
- not having enough resources to get the work done
- dealing with setbacks and changes.

Emotional intelligence is crucial for those in management or leadership positions. Leadership works through emotion[124], not just logic. EQ can also help you as outlined below:

3. How to enhance your emotional intelligence

There are a variety of resources available to help you enhance your emotional intelligence[125].

However, it is best to starting with an assessment of your current emotional intelligence. There are simple and free tests[126]. However, you will obtain substantially more benefit from using more comprehensive and informative assessments such as the or the ESCI 360[127] test based on the twelve factors in the table above, or the EQ-i 2.0[128] test which measures the following factors as shown in the table below:

EQ FACTOR	ABILITY ASSESSED
Self-Perception	
Self-awareness	awareness/understanding of feelings and impact
Self-regard	respect strengths and weaknesses
Self-actualisation	improve and pursue objectives
Self-Expression	
Emotional expression	express feelings verbally and non-verbally
Independence	self-directed and free of dependence on others
Assertiveness	express feelings, thoughts, beliefs in non-destructive way
Interpersonal	
Interpersonal relationships	develop and maintain mutually satisfying relationships
Empathy	recognise, understand, and appreciate feelings of others
Social responsibility	contribute to society and welfare of others
Decision Making	
Impulse control	resist or delay an impulse, drive, or temptation to act
Reality testing	remain objective by seeing things as they really are
Problem solving	solve problems with emotions involved

	using emotions
Stress Management	
Flexibility	adapt feelings, thinking and behaviour to change
Stress tolerance	effectively cope with stressful or difficult situations
Optimism	hopeful and resilient despite setbacks
Additional	
Happiness	feel satisfied with yourself, others, and life in general

Simply understanding the different factors involved in emotional intelligence can help inform what you need to focus on to enhance your EQ. However, it will help if you undertake a formal assessment, ideally involving input from others that know you professionally or personally.

Once you have identified which areas you might be deficient in, especially if these are causing problems for you in your life or work, then you can try to address these yourself. However, it may be necessary to seek help from accredited coaches or other professionals to enhance these aspects of your EQ.

Emotional intelligence is somewhat unique, and plays a special role in the Framework, in that it involves a combination of different qualities and capabilities. Some of these, such as optimism and interpersonal relations, I have not called out as separate components of the Framework, whereas I have called out others such as empathy and adaptability. The ones that I have included in the Framework are the most crucial ones for the purpose of becoming a T-Shaped Lawyer.

CHAPTER 5

T-SHAPED LAWYER KNOWLEDGE

Knowledge is an area that is often overlooked in discussions about what lawyers need to survive and thrive in this ever-changing landscape. It is not all about new skills, as some might have you believe.

You know that legal knowledge is crucial to you as a lawyer to use in conjunction with legal skills to do excellent legal work. So too, a range of business knowledge will greatly enhance your ability to be a T-Shaped Lawyer who can provide excellent business advice and do excellent business work.

That said, as I mentioned in the first book, the fact that you may not have an extensive business knowledge currently does not prevent you from starting to do this type of work immediately. Although you may not think so, you already have acquired a level of business knowledge and actually doing business work is one terrific way in which you can further develop that knowledge.

Also, as Satya Nadella, the CEO of Microsoft, said *'don't be a know-it-all. Be a learn-it-all'*. Many lawyers act like a know-it-all because they believe that this will impress clients and other lawyers. Ironically, there is nothing more impressive than someone who freely admits that they do not know about something and then they take the opportunity to learn about it.

T-Shaped Lawyers do not try to flaunt their existing knowledge. Rather they try to broaden their knowledge and then to use it to provide new insights and add more value. They are 'learn-it-alls,' as I shall explain in more detail later in the book.

In one sense learning about all types of things is a good thing. However, there are certain categories of business knowledge, more so than others, that will help you to do better legal work and to do internal and client business work. If you have a Businessperson Mindset, then developing this knowledge will not be difficult. It will be something you will do willingly and enjoy.

These important areas of knowledge are depicted in the Framework below and briefly explained in the following sections of this chapter together with some suggestions for how to enhance these areas continually over time. These suggestions will relate to steps you can take as individual lawyers[129].

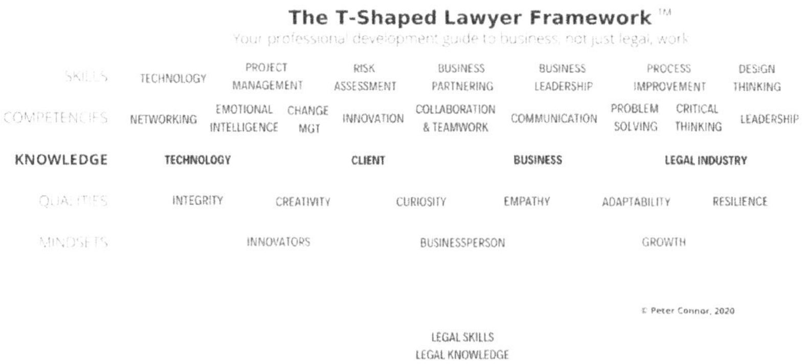

A. Business Knowledge

The first area of relevant knowledge is knowledge of business in general. I am often surprised at how little many corporate lawyers know about what is happening in the business world. If you are a corporate lawyer then, even if you only do legal work, a basic knowledge of business is very important.

To be a different lawyer, a T-Shaped Lawyer, who also provides business input and does business work, developing a broader knowledge of business becomes even more important. Frankly, if you have the necessary Businessperson Mindset then an interest in business, and a hunger to know more about it, will follow quite naturally.

1. What do you need to know about business?

At the very least it is important that you have a basic understanding of:

- macroeconomics[130]
- microeconomics[131]
- finance and capital markets[132]
- the latest global and local economic and financial news[133]
- key business trends such as outsourcing, gig economy and digital transformation.

In addition to this general business knowledge, it is especially important to develop an even deeper level of knowledge about your client's industry. In other words, allocate more time to following the business trends relevant to your client's industry than other industries so that you can at least:

- talk about the general themes, priorities, and issues applicable to that industry.
- identify the key historical and emerging competitors and discuss their respective financial and strategic position.

It is extremely helpful for you to also develop an understanding of the technology business even if your client is not in that industry. The reason for this is that technology is so pervasive that it impacts every industry. Increasingly, every business is looking at how they can transform their business to become a technology business. Technology business knowledge is discussed below.

2. How to enhance your business knowledge

There are links above and here[134] for further study to develop your knowledge in the business world in general. It is also helpful to regularly follow business news that will keep you up to date with developments but also, over time, fill in gaps in your business knowledge.

If you work in-house, then every day is an opportunity to enhance your business knowledge if you pay attention to what your business and functional colleagues are saying. For law firm lawyers there is also an extremely helpful book[135] written on the topic of industry knowledge and specialisation. Do not be afraid to ask your clients for suggestions for how you can develop industry specific knowledge and they will typically be impressed that you have asked them.

B. Knowledge of your Client's Business

To provide commercial pragmatic legal advice it is necessary for lawyers to understand not just business in general but your client's business in particular. This need becomes even more acute if you want to be a T-Shaped Lawyer and to do client business work.

Despite that need, many in-house lawyers have a rather superficial and limited knowledge of the business of their corporations often because they are too busy with the legal tasks to take the time to become better informed. Also, it is a common complaint of in-house lawyers and business clients that their legal advisers in firms do not sufficiently understand their business. Granted it is not possible for every lawyer working in a firm to have as deep a knowledge of every client's business as those working in-house. However, it is possible, and highly desirable, for law firm lawyers to have a sound understanding at least for your key clients.

Another point worth remembering is that if you work in a law firm there is often an additional 'client' for you to consider – the inhouse legal department and the in-house lawyers with whom you interact.

1. What do you need to know about your client's business

It is crucial to highlight that for all corporate lawyers there are two levels of knowledge required of your client: macro or

organisational knowledge, on the one hand and micro or individual knowledge on the other hand.

i. Macro or organisational knowledge

When most people think and talk about understanding your client, they are typically referring to what I call a 'macro' level of understanding. In other words, they are talking about *the business of the company.*

In broad terms it is important for you to keep current on, at least, the following areas of the company's business:

- background of the relevant industry. Who are the key competitors? What are the trends, challenges, and opportunities in that industry?
- key products and services offered.
- how and where are these products developed and produced.
- how and where are the products and services marketed and sold.
- who are the key members of management and the functional leaders.
- the organisation structure of the business.
- the financial situation including revenue models, profitability, cash flow and balance sheet.
- key priorities, challenges, and strategies.
- major policies and procedures.

That said, the nature and extent of knowledge required will vary depending on who you interact with on a regular basis and the business functions that you support. So, for example, someone who supports or interacts with the product development group needs to have a deeper understanding about that aspect of the business, whereas a lawyer who supports or interacts with sales and marketing functions would need a deeper understanding of that aspect.

ii. Micro or individual knowledge

A micro level of knowledge means you understand what *the individual executives* that you interact with do in their work, the challenges they face and even the emotional issues involved. This more granular level of understanding of your client is crucial for innovation, design thinking and for more advanced client business work.

Very few lawyers have a micro understanding of their clients and enhancing this area of knowledge, at least for your key clients, can pay huge dividends.

2. How to enhance your macro and micro knowledge of your clients

There are a variety of ways to obtain a better macro level of knowledge including the following:

- Read publicly available information such as news, business magazines, websites, annual reports, press releases or analyst reports.

- If you have access to internal information, take the time to look at the intranet and read any updates/announcements.
- If you have access to key company executives, talk to them as part of your networking.
- If you work in a firm and do not have access to executives, ask your in-house lawyer contacts. They will usually be pleased and impressed that you take the time to better understand the business.
- Use technology[136] to curate information feeds to you.

When it comes to a micro level of knowledge, there is no substitute for simply observing your customers and talking to them about their work. There are a variety of tools to help you do this including design thinking and various innovation tools that I use in my workshops.

C. Technology Knowledge

In a world where technology has already made such a significant impact on you and your work, and promises to continue to do so more and more, at least a basic knowledge of technology is imperative for every lawyer.

Some of those reading this book will be well versed in technology and this section of the book may be a bit basic for you. However, technology is an area that intimidates many lawyers and as a result they make little to no effort to try to understand it. It is not difficult to gain and maintain some level of knowledge about technology that will help you to, at least, understand how technology can impact you and your work.

1. What do you need to know about technology?

To start with, it is important to distinguish between technology in general and legal technology (also known as LegalTech).

i. LegalTech

The prevailing focus in the legal industry on all things legal that I highlighted in relation to skills in the Framework, also applies to the area of technology knowledge. Most of the discussion in the legal industry about technology is in fact about legal technology or LegalTech. Legal technology is technology primarily for use by legal departments and firms. No doubt your department or firm will use such technology and it is important for you to understand and, where appropriate, use it.

It is helpful to have a basic level of knowledge about the current and emerging legal technologies and there are a variety of resources available to enhance your knowledge[137]. However, if this is not an area of interest for you, it is not essential for you to have a deep understanding of LegalTech because there will undoubtedly be others in your department and firm who do.

Developing a basic understanding of LegalTech is one thing, but understanding technology in general is even more important for all corporate lawyers. The reason for this is because, as I suggested in the discussion on digital skills, the key idea of a T-Shaped Lawyer is to apply technology for clients, not just use it internally in the legal department or firm.

ii. Technology in general

The topic of technology, and the technology industry, is vast and constantly in a state of extreme flux. As a result, it can sometimes feel overwhelming, and difficult to understand, if you do not work in that industry.

However, because technology is now so integral to every business, it is crucial that every lawyer develop, and maintain, at least a basic understanding of the technology industry including the following areas:

- The leading technology companies, such as Google, Microsoft, Facebook, Amazon and their products and service offerings.
- The emerging technology companies such as Open AI.

- 'Non-technology' businesses that are in fact technology businesses such as Airbnb, Netflix, and Uber.
- Key technology and technology concepts such as SaaS (software as a service), hosting, cloud computing, apps, bots, platforms v point products, no-code software, API (application programming interface), machine learning, MVP (minimum viable product), blockchain, UI (user interface), and artificial intelligence including generative AI.

For most lawyers, it is not so important that you understand technology at a technical level but rather than you understand it at a business level. In other words, it is not essential to be able to necessarily use these technologies to develop products. However, it useful to know:

- what these core technologies are
- how they are being used by businesses and
- how they could be used by you and your legal department, firm, or company.

There are various levels of knowledge in this area. The minimum level of knowledge is so that you can understand when your business clients discuss these topics. Higher levels of knowledge would allow you to identify opportunities to utilise different technologies and then work with technical experts to make or buy these as explained in the technology skills section of this book.

2. How to enhance your technology knowledge

There are a multitude of resources to help you develop and maintain your technology knowledge including those in the reference notes[138]. You could do any number of courses to accelerate your learning in this area. However, often the most practical way to expand your technology knowledge is to do so progressively over time as and when a technology topic comes to your attention.

Also, another wonderful, but frequently overlooked, source for learning about technology are the technology experts who work in your company or firm. They are typically very willing to help you develop your technology knowledge especially if you do it in conjunction with other colleagues.

D. Legal industry Knowledge

The final area of knowledge highlighted in the T-Shaped Lawyer Framework is knowledge of the legal industry – the industry that you work in.

We are not talking here about knowledge of the law. Rather we are talking about knowledge of the business of law. We are also not talking here about knowledge of your legal department or firm in isolation. Rather we are talking about knowledge of the rapidly evolving ecosystem of all the various players involved in your country, and other countries, in the provision of legal services and products.

I am frequently amazed at how unaware most corporate lawyers are about the changes and trends in the corporate legal industry. You would think that the one thing every lawyer would be acutely interested in is their own industry.

Maybe the reason that they are not aware of what is going on in the industry is because they are too busy with their daily tasks. Or perhaps it is because, in the past, you could possibly get away with not paying attention because the industry changes were not that significant or frequent to impact every lawyer. If you are reading this book, then you are probably not one of those lawyers. Likely you understand that keeping abreast of these changes and trends is key to your professional development, your work, and your career choices.

1. What knowledge do you need about the corporate legal industry?

In the first chapter of the first book, I provided a comprehensive outline of the many different areas of relevant knowledge in the industry. I encourage you to read that chapter to learn about these main areas of knowledge and to give you an overview of some of the key changes and trends.

To stay abreast of these changes in future, you should find sustainable ways to regularly follow the changes in the industry.

2. How to enhance your legal industry knowledge

Keeping up to date with the constant changes in the legal industry is not easy because there is no one convenient source of truth and knowledge. There are however several different ways for you to keep your legal industry knowledge current, and at the same time facilitate networking, including the following:

- **Conferences** are a popular and effective way of staying in touch with changes in the law and in the industry. They are also useful networking opportunities. However, many conferences do tend to have the same people saying the same things. So, it is important to assess whether each conference is going to provide you with new insights and not rely just on conferences as your primary source of this knowledge.
- **LinkedIn** and other social media offer excellent ways to stay in touch with the latest developments. If you regularly check in on LinkedIn, you will soon realise which individuals are the

thought leaders and most generous with sharing developments in the industry. You can connect, or at least follow, these people to keep abreast of changes in the industry. However, it does require the discipline of checking in on a regular basis.

- **Webinars** featuring industry thought leaders are readily available, often for free, from associations, legal communities, law firms, legal tech companies and alternative service providers. Look out for these and choose ones that appear to offer genuine thought leadership.
- **Books and articles** are published on a frequent basis by publishers like Legal Business World and GlobeLawandBusiness, by associations, like ACC Docket, and by other organisations like Thomson Reuters or Lexis Nexis. I have referenced some useful books and authors in this book and in the first book.
- **Talk and interact** with other people in your network who do follow the changes closely.

Whatever means you use to enhance your knowledge of the legal industry, it is very important to apply critical thinking to assess what is said and written by others. This will allow you to filter for relevance, credibility, accuracy, logic, significance, bias, and any vested interests. For example:

- most commentary is about law firms and lawyers working there. If you are working as an in-house lawyer, comments about 'lawyers' may not apply to you in the same way, or at all, given the gap between these two roles that I referred to in my first book.

- there are many who claim to be experts but who in fact have had very little relevant experience. Consider this factor when you consider what these people say.
- there is so much written and said that it can be overwhelming to decide what to spend your time focussing on. It is important to be able to quickly distinguish between 'noise', on the one hand, and genuinely insightful commentary that helps you to achieve your goals and objectives, on the other hand. As Adam Grant says, *'don't read what you like to hear, read what makes you think hard'.*
- technology attracts a disproportionate amount of coverage. It is, of course, an important topic. However, logic should tell you that technology is one means to an end and that there are many other topics that you should follow.
- understandably, some commentators are biased and have a vested interest in a particular narrative that supports their business. Do not necessarily ignore those commentators but take that bias and interest into account when you are listening to or reading what they say.

Like the other components of the T-Shaped Lawyer Framework, the idea is not to rush out and prioritise uplevelling your knowledge over any of the other Framework areas. It is also not necessary to be an expert in any of these areas of knowledge unless you have an inherent interest in that area.

Remember that a T-Shaped Lawyer is an expert generalist. That means that your aim, over time, is to develop your knowledge so that you become, and remain, generally aware of these areas.

One very helpful tip is that if you work with others in a legal department or firm, then you can each take responsibility to take the lead in different categories of knowledge. The lead person can share updates with others in the team and save everyone some time. That said, every lawyer should take personal responsibility to ensure they have the necessary general knowledge and awareness. This should follow automatically if adopt a Businessperson Mindset and you become a 'learn-it-all' as explained later in the book.

CHAPTER 6

T-SHAPED LAWYER QUALITIES

Qualities are personal attributes that determine your nature and influence your thinking and behaviour in work and in other aspects of your life. Qualities are like mindsets in that they:

- can help, or hinder, your work performance.
- are to some extent innate but can be acquired or developed.
- need to be combined with skills and knowledge to produce work outcomes.
- are insufficient on their own to transform your way of working but, without them, it would be difficult to do so.

The fundamental difference between mindsets and qualities is that mindsets are the way you think or perceive of yourself, whereas qualities are the way you really are. For that reason, your work colleagues and friends may not know your mindsets, but they will more readily be able to see your qualities.

There are, of course, many different personal qualities and it may be that any number of these qualities may hindering your work performance. In the notes[139] I have included references to a few general personality tests which may be useful.

However, in my experience there are certain qualities that are particularly relevant to becoming a T-Shaped lawyer and to doing client business work. It is just these qualities that I shall focus on in this book as highlighted in the Framework below.

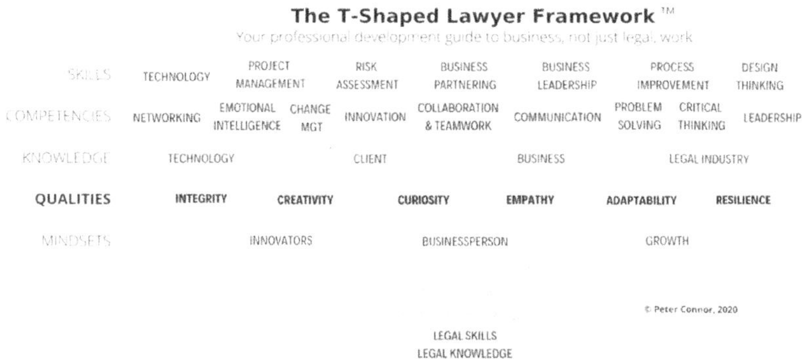

For the purposes of this book, my aim is to provide you with a basic level of understanding of these qualities, explain how they can be relevant to transforming your work and provide you with some suggestions and resources to enhance these qualities.

Your objective should be to:

- understand to what extent you have these qualities, or not.
- identify when a lack of one of these qualities is impeding your ability to be an effective T-Shaped Lawyer and, in such cases, to incorporate a focus on enhancing this quality into your development plans.
- be generally mindful of these qualities and consciously develop them in the context of your work and using new skills.

A. Curiosity

Curiosity is an increasingly valued quality in the workplace and is a critical quality to be a T-Shaped Lawyer. There are many reasons for this including:

- it enhances your engagement at work.
- it is the key to lifelong learning and facilitates development of all T-Shaped capabilities.
- it is critical for innovation.
- it helps you to spot opportunities to add value especially in relation to internal business work and for client business work.

1. What is curiosity?

Curiosity can be defined as *'the impulse to seek new information and experiences and to explore novel possibilities[140]'*.

In its Curiosity Report[141], Merck identified four dimensions to curiosity as shown below.

Inquisitiveness	Creativity in problem solving
Openness to other ideas	Distress tolerance

*'**Inquisitiveness** refers to how a person reacts in response to feeling curious and includes exploratory behavior like freely asking questions **and thinking and acting beyond one's own job requirements**.*

***Creativity in problem solving** can be thought of as a desire or willingness to challenge the status quo and an ability to identify new approaches to problem solving.*

***Openness to other ideas** can be defined as preferring a variety of experiences, being attentive to the world, and open to new ideas, whether they come from oneself or from others.*

***Distress tolerance** allows a person to take risks, to persevere and to approach the new and unfamiliar without fear. No matter how inquisitive, creative, and open a person might be, they may find it difficult-to-impossible to ever express their curiosity without a significant tolerance for distress. Its importance in the role of curiosity cannot be understated. Distress tolerance tends to determine whether that person will act on his or her curiosity in a meaningful way, or instead become discouraged and move on'*[142].

Understanding these dimensions helps to inform the many ways that you as an individual can enhance your curiosity.

2. How to enhance your curiosity

In addition to focussing on enhancing each of the four dimensions, below are a few suggestions for how you can develop your curiosity in a professional context:

- **Adopt the T-Shaped Lawyer Mindsets.** If you have the Businessperson, Growth, and Innovators mindsets then you will almost certainly be highly curious. Your curiosity will naturally grow with little conscious effort. Conversely, if you do not have these mindsets, it will be difficult to develop your curiosity. It will feel like you are forcing yourself and your efforts to be more curious will likely not be sustainable.
- **Resist making assumptions based on what you know.** Keep an open mind and do not assume that something must be a certain way just because it has always been that way.
- **Question everything – ask why**. Children constantly ask questions if they do not understand something without any fear of what others might think of them. Most adults lose that freedom to be inquisitive for a variety of reasons. Try to rediscover that inner child. Take the time to reflect on things rather than just doing tasks. Challenge the status quo. Learn how to ask good questions[143]. Use rhetorical questions. Ask *'what if'* and *'how might we'* to explore new ways of doing things.
- **Seek out novel experiences.** One of the best ways to learn and satisfy your thirst for new information and experiences is to challenge yourself and **actively look for opportunities to get 'out of your comfort zone'**. It could be as simple as getting out of your normal work environment and seeing new work environments in or out of your workplace. Alternatively, you might try a new role or volunteering for a project whether you have sufficient skills or knowledge or not.
- **Connect with others.** Talking to people from diverse backgrounds can help you to learn new things and foster

curiosity especially if you take a real interest in what they do and say.

- **Read widely.** If you are curious then you will automatically tend to read widely and not just about matters directly relevant to your work. Reading widely, taking online courses, and listening to podcasts on a wide range of topics will feed your hunger to learn and will fuel your curiosity even further.
- **Face your fears.** It is important to understand what is your 'distress tolerance' and try to identify, and overcome, what if any factors hinder your ability to act on your curiosity. It may be that you do not want to sound silly or ill-informed especially in the company of your legal or business colleagues. Perhaps you lack confidence in your abilities or become uncomfortable when you are in an unfamiliar situation. Think about what is stopping you from asking questions and trying new things and try to address these underlying causes.

If you are reading this book, then there is a high probability that you are already quite curious. Based on my interactions with thousands of lawyers all over the world, I can assure you that not all lawyers are curious. That has not necessarily been a problem for them in being just a lawyer and doing just legal work.

However, to be a T-Shaped Lawyer who also provides business input and business advice, curiosity becomes far more important. Curiosity is really a foundational quality for that purpose because it facilitates the acquisition of the broad range of knowledge, skills and competencies required. Also, it helps you to spot new ways to add value for your clients and to identify and address unseen problems and opportunities. Finally, curiosity is central to the next quality - creativity.

B. Creativity

Creative thinking has been rated the single most important trait by the World Economic Forum in its latest Future of Jobs Report[144]. Lawyers do not in general have a reputation for being creative. That may be because many lawyers are risk averse, tend to follow the tried and tested way of doing things, and are better at spotting problems than finding solutions.

However, you do not need to be a 'creative type', such as an artist or musician, to be creative in your work. In fact, quite a few lawyers can be very creative in relation to legal work, for example, when it comes to structuring transactions to avoid, or minimise, legal risk.

To be a T-Shaped Lawyer, the point is to be creative not just in relation to legal advice or legal work but also in relation to business advice and business work. This is especially important when you try to find solutions for unseen business problems and opportunities as part of business leadership.

1. What is creativity?

Creativity is the ability to come up with new ideas and turn them into reality. Almost always these new ideas will arise by combining existing ideas to create something useful that has never been there before. It involves the capacity to see things in new and unique ways, to make connections between seemingly unrelated concepts, and to break free from conventional ways of thinking.

'Creativity is characterised by the ability to perceive the world in new ways, to find hidden patterns, to make connections between seemingly unrelated phenomena, and to generate solutions. Creativity involves two processes: thinking, then producing.

Creativity is a combinatorial force: it's our ability to tap into our 'inner' pool of resources – knowledge, insight, information, inspiration and all the fragments populating our minds – that we've accumulated over the years just by being present and alive and awake to the world and to combine them in extraordinary new ways[145]'.

2. How to enhance your creativity

There are countless books on how to enhance your creativity[146] but below are a few suggestions:

- Carve out time away from your daily work and personal tasks to reflect, to think and to daydream. It may be on the commute to work, on an airplane or by taking a short break from work. If you are constantly busy doing urgent things, then it is difficult for you to see things from a new perspective.
- Change your work environment. If you constantly work in the same environment, you will tend to see things in the same way.
- Seek inspiration from diverse sources such as sport, art, music, nature, and the business world.
- It is acceptable to build on the ideas of others, provided you acknowledge their work. It is rare to come up with an idea that does not derive from an existing idea.

- Use analogy/analogical thinking which is characterised by extrapolations from the familiar to the unfamiliar, rather than using formal logic or consecutive reasoning.
- Spend time thinking about a problem if it is a complex one. Avoid jumping to conclusions or solutions because you may miss truly breakthrough ideas.
- Identify what characteristics might be blocking your creativity and try to change these behaviours. For example, creativity stiflers include:

    - believing that you are always right
    - being negative and criticising the ideas of others
    - striving for perfection
    - not being open to criticism
    - unwillingness to let go of your idea if it is not practical or there is a better idea
    - believing that you are not creative.

- Take risks, try new things, experiment and be OK with failures.
- Collaborate – be willing to work in teams and bounce your ideas off others.
- Be curious – constantly ask '*why*' and '*what if*'.
- Use various techniques and tools such as design thinking, brainstorming and mind mapping. Also apply your problem solving competency as explained earlier in the book.

Becoming a T-Shaped Lawyer, by using the Framework to develop and do business work, also helps you to be more creative. The wider your knowledge, capabilities, and experience, the easier it is to be creative because you have 'more dots' to connect. However, this only works if you have a Businessperson Mindset.

Finally, research has also shown that empathy tends to facilitate creativity. Empathy is the next quality in the Framework, and it is discussed below.

C. Empathy

Empathy is a key component of emotional intelligence. However, it is worthy of separate mention in the T-Shaped Lawyer Framework because it is also extremely important in other ways.

When most people think of using empathy in a work context, they think of using it to understand and feel the personal problems of a work colleague. That is an important application of empathy, especially for managers and leaders, who want to help their colleagues overcome any personal problems or achieve their personal objectives.

However, empathy can, and should, also be used by lawyers in a different context – to understand the personal motivations, and the business problems or objectives, of your clients and even third parties with whom you are doing business. This is an application of this quality in line with the vision of being a T-Shaped Lawyer and helping the business not just the legal department or firm. So, for example, empathy in this context:

- helps you to understand why your client, or a third party, is behaving a certain way and informs what you might do, taking that into account, to achieve the desired outcome.
- enables a truly client centric approach to your work.
- is the key to innovation for clients and is critical to the skill of design thinking.
- is essential to becoming a T-Shaped Lawyer because it is difficult, if not impossible, to be a businessperson and do

business work if you cannot, at least, put yourself in the shoes of the business and see things from their perspective.

Despite the importance of empathy for corporate lawyers, studies have shown that most lawyers have relatively low levels of empathy. That conclusion is also consistent with my own observations of hundreds of lawyers when conducting design thinking workshops or training.

Why might many lawyers have low levels of empathy?

Some have suggested that training to 'think like a lawyer' results in a focus on thinking, not feeling. In the desire to be dispassionate, and not let emotions get in the way of objectivity or critical thinking, perhaps many lawyers have lost some degree of empathy. I also believe that the default vision of being better lawyers, results in an inward, not an outward, focus where there is no premium attached to empathy. **As Daniel Goldman has pointed out, in an age of introspection, which is important for self-awareness, becoming more empathetic requires a conscious focus on '*outrospection*'.**

If you believe, as I do, that enhancing your empathy levels is important than a great place to start is to have a clear understanding of what this quality means.

1. What is empathy?

Empathy is not the same thing as sympathy. It is not about feeling sorry for someone. Rather it is the ability to use your imagination to understand and, in some cases, share the feelings of others.

Daniel Goldman[147] refers to three different types of empathy:

i. Cognitive empathy

Cognitive empathy is the ability to understand someone else's perspective. To put yourself in their shoes and to see things from their perspective but not necessarily engaging with their emotions. **Cognitive empathy is also referred to as empathy by thought rather than by feeling or '*head to heart*'.**

ii. Emotional empathy

Emotional empathy goes beyond cognitive empathy. It involves the ability to feel what others feel, to connect to their emotions and so understand them at a deeper level. **It is also known as affective empathy or '*heart to heart*'.**

This form of empathy is useful when it comes to interpersonal relationships because it enables a very close connection and rapport. It is especially important for anyone working in the caring roles like nurses. It is also helpful to be able to respond to friends and co-workers who might need help and, as such, is useful for those in leadership or management positions.

However, there is a risk to unchecked emotional empathy. You may become overwhelmed by those emotions and unable to respond appropriately. Self-management becomes critical here to regulate those feelings and to avoid exhaustion and burnout.

iii. Compassionate Empathy

Compassionate empathy, or empathetic concern, is the most active form of empathy. **It involves not only having concern for another person, and sharing their emotional pain, but also taking, or helping others to take, practical steps to resolve the problem or improve the situation.**

How empathy is relevant to your work as a corporate lawyer

Understanding the different forms of empathy is important because you may be strong in one form but not in another. Ideally you want to have high levels of all forms of empathy.

However, not all forms of empathy are appropriate for all situations in your work as a corporate lawyer. It depends on the context. For example:

- For a non-corporate lawyer, emotional and compassionate empathy in relation to clients is important because they typically advise individuals on very personal matters often in times of distress.
- Emotional and compassionate empathy are typically less important for you as a corporate lawyer because you are advising business or legal executives about business matters and usually without any personal distress. Indeed, it may not be appropriate or desirable to get too emotionally involved with your business clients and may, in extreme cases, adversely impact your work. **Cognitive empathy is the most important and relevant form of empathy for corporate lawyers in relation to legal and, especially, business advice.**

- **However, that is not to say that emotional and compassionate empathy are not important for corporate lawyers.** These forms of empathy are important where, for example, there is some underlying emotion involved in a particular situation and you need to factor that into your advice or work. Emotional and compassionate empathy are also crucial for leaders and managers to help your colleagues succeed and overcome any personal difficulties they may be experiencing.

2. How to enhance your empathy

It helps to start with an objective assessment of your current levels of all forms of empathy. You can ask those you trust for their views on your empathy levels and there are also various empathy assessment tests[148] available.

There is no shortage of guidance[149] to help you develop your empathy levels. **One general way to enhance empathy is to practise mindfulness**. Mindfulness helps empathy because it is all about being present and focussing on those who you are with.

As a corporate lawyer the primary opportunity for you to show, and practise, empathy is in your interactions with clients and colleagues. Here are a few practical suggestions for these interactions:

- **Listen.** To truly empathise with someone, you must be able to really listen to what they are saying. *Active listening* involves saying something to acknowledge that you have heard what is being said. Paraphrasing the key points is often a useful technique.

- **Ask good questions**. One of the best, and simplest, ways to empathise with someone is to ask good questions. Good questions are not just ones to extract the facts you need. If you are being empathetic, good questions may include questions about their personal life or their feelings and ideally build on something they have said before. This tells that person that you were listening and remembered what they said. That builds rapport and trust and is likely to lead to them opening up even more.
- **Observe**. Sometimes people say one thing and do something completely different. To truly understand someone, carefully watch what they do to check that what they have told you corresponds with their behaviour.
- **Don't rush**. Lawyers tend to rush or interrupt clients to extract the facts as quickly as possible or to give their opinion. Give someone time and space to talk and sometimes the important information is revealed later in the conversation.
- **Delay judgement**. Again, lawyers are quick to make a judgement. Being empathetic involves taking time to really consider the situation before you come to any conclusions.
- **Don't make it about you**. You may think sharing an experience you see as comparable is being empathetic. However, making such a comparison or judgement, typically breaks the feeling of connection. Don't be a *conversational narcissist* – someone who always brings the conversation back to themselves.
- **Be yourself**. Important to be authentic and respond accordingly. Make sure your responses are human but sincere.

Thankfully there has been a lot of focus in recent times on the importance of empathy in the legal profession. Just remember the different forms of empathy and how you can develop and use them in different contexts. Doing so will improve your personal and professional lives and help you to be a T-Shaped Lawyer.

D. Adaptability

Adaptability may be the single most critical quality of all, especially in a VUCA world of constant and discontinuous change[150].

'The slowest rate of change for the rest of your life is right now'[151]. *'When everything starts shifting so quickly, we have to become adept at adapting...the ability to adapt is our key advantage.*[152]*'*

Heather McGowan and Chris Shipley, the authors of *The Adaptation Advantage*[153], **assert that for individuals and organisations to thrive in the future of work, the key is learning, unlearning and adaptation.**

If you are reading this book, then it is likely that you understand the importance of adaptability and are willing to adapt. Being open to change is one thing but knowing how to change is quite another thing, as this book attempts to explain.

1. What is adaptability?

Adaptability is the ability to adjust as a result, or in anticipation, of changed circumstances. That adaptation could be to yourself, it could be to your team, and/or it could be to your circumstances.

As Bernard Shaw said *'the reasonable man adapts to the changed world; the unreasonable man tries to adapt the world to himself. All progress depends on the unreasonable man'*. **In other words, you should not only try to manage change but also to lead**

change in yourself, your team and your organisation as explained in this book.

In that sense adaptability is a fundamental quality that underlies your ability to become a T-Shaped Lawyer: to act as a leader; to innovate within your department or firm and for the client organisation; to engage in internal business work and, in particular, business leadership work.

2. How to enhance your adaptability

Like other qualities, the starting point is to understand the extent to which you are, or are not, adaptable. The table below should provide you with a rough indication.

Adaptive person	Non-adaptive person
Excited about change	Anxious/fearful about change
Optimistic about change	Sees change as a threat
Open to new possibilities	Prefer to stick to old habits and ways of working
Comfortable in changing/ unpredictable environments	Can be paralysed by change
Actively contributes to change	Actively or passively resists change

Another simple way to ascertain the extent to which you are adaptable is to ask people you trust to provide their view on your adaptability. However, there are a variety of more sophisticated ways[154] to measure what is known as your adaptability quotient or AQ.

Once you have a sense of your adaptability it is helpful to consider what, if any factors, are hindering your adaptability.

As I pointed out in the discussion on the Businessperson Mindset, one common and significant obstacle to adaptability is your identity as a lawyer. You have spent a lot of time, money, and effort to become a lawyer and, in many cases, **being a lawyer is a very significant part of your personal identity**. **Whilst that is understandable, it is important to recognise that this identity may be an obstacle to you adapting yourself and your work.**

As McGowan and Shipley state in *The Adaptation Advantage*[155]*:*

'To successfully learn and adapt, we have to be willing to ***let go of 'the way we have always done it'*** *and equally, and more difficultly,* ***'who we think we are'****...that identity plays a crucial role as a social signal and is, in many cases, the basis for self-esteem. It is also an anchor that makes the necessary re-imagining of work much, much, harder than it needs to be. It is the barrier to making the crossing from the past of work to the future of work. But cross it we must. The ability to adapt is our key advantage.* ***The first step to seizing that advantage is letting go of our professional identity, and in letting go, tapping into our imaginations to re-imagine ourselves and our work.'***

Letting go of your identity as a lawyer does not mean that you should not be proud of the fact that you are a lawyer. It also does not mean that you need to stop thinking of yourself as a lawyer. Rather it means not defining yourself solely as a lawyer. Adopting a Businessperson Mindset is a simple and effective way to 'let go' of your identity as a lawyer. This involves thinking of yourself as *more than* just a lawyer, in other words **also** as a businessperson.

If we can do that then we can, as the authors state, *'re-imagine ourselves and our work'* which is precisely what we have done with the idea of a T-Shaped Lawyer and the idea of doing business work not just legal work.

Once you understand your current ability to adapt, there are a few things you can do to enhance your adaptability as explained in *The Adaptation Advantage*[156].

Here are some other factors to consider:

- **Learning.** Continuous learning and adaptability go hand in hand. You need to take responsibility for your lifelong learning as I will explain in more detail later in the book.
- **Positive Mindset.** It is important to try to see change as an opportunity not a threat. Adopting this positive perspective will help you to be more adaptable.
- **Unlearning.** To learn new ways, you often need to unlearn the old ways of working. This applies particularly to business partnering because it involves doing something familiar - advising clients - in a new way.
- **Courage.** Having the courage to experiment with new ways of working is one of the keys to adaptability. Adopting the T-Shaped Lawyer vision, and using the T-Shaped Lawyer

Framework as the basis of your professional development, should give you greater confidence and courage to adapt to new ways of working and new situations.

- **Practice**. The best way to become more adaptable is to put yourself in positions where you are outside your comfort zone. Actively search out projects and new roles where they will give you an opportunity to learn.

To sum up, to become a T-Shaped Lawyer and to do client work requires adaptability. It requires letting go of your identity as a lawyer, unlearning some of the ways you have done things before, and learning new ways of doing things. If you can do that and develop your self-awareness and other components of the T-Shaped Lawyer Framework, you will, at the same time, enhance your adaptability in general. It is a virtuous circle.

Becoming more adaptable also enhances your resilience. For example, adapting to become a T-Shaped Lawyer means you are less reliant on one specific thing – doing legal work – and, because of your broader capabilities, more able to contribute to your firm or company in other ways. Resilience is the next quality in the Framework and is discussed in the next section.

E. Resilience

Resilience is one of the top three most highly rated qualities in the workplace in the latest World Economic Forum Report[157]. One of the reasons for that is because, in a world of rapid and discontinuous change, people are going to experience more serious and more frequent setbacks and stress in their lives and careers. Employers want people who can cope with this stress and these setbacks. Of course, resilience is just as important from the perspective of individuals.

Research[158] into the lawyer personality has revealed that 90% of lawyers score in the bottom half of the scale on resilience. That is a problem for those individuals because a lack of resilience can contribute to burnout, various mental health issues and frustrate their attempts to progress and thrive in their personal and professional lives. It is also a problem for legal departments and firms because low resilient people are likely to underperform and may also adversely impact team moral.

1. What is resilience?

'Resilience describes the capacity to adapt effectively to life adversity with a short-lived downturn in functioning[159]'. In other words, resilience involves the ability to cope with changing demands and circumstances and to 'bounce back' in the face of this adversity.

The following may be indicators of low resilience or even burnout[160]:

- Feeling like a victim or feeling powerless

- Being easily wounded by criticism, rejection, or setbacks
- Being excessively irritable or emotional
- Becoming less tolerant of others
- Resenting the demands placed on you by others
- Losing hope and seeing everything as lacking meaning
- Using unhealthy coping mechanisms

2. How to enhance resilience

The starting point to enhance your resilience level should be to assess it. Assessment is worthwhile for all qualities and other components of the framework. However, it is especially important to understand your resilience level because you want to know if you have a lack of resilience before problems emerge. There are many ways to measure your resilience[161] and to assess whether you are suffering from burnout[162].

Once you know your current level of resilience there are many different resources[163] available to help you enhance your resilience and reduce the risk of burnout. A detailed coverage of this topic is beyond the scope of this book. However below are some thoughts to give you a general indication of some ways to enhance resilience.

There are obviously lots of things outside of your control that may impact you adversely including, for example, what your manager thinks of you, what happens to your company or firm, or what will happen in the future because of technology changes.

In general, it helps to focus on the things that are within your control and that includes your:

- **Mindset**. How you react to setbacks is often a question of how you view a situation or development. You may not be able to control the situation, but you do have a choice over how you view it. You can choose to look at things from a negative perspective, feeling like you are a victim, and giving up hope. Alternatively, **if you can adopt a positive mindset and be optimistic about the future, you are more likely to be able to bounce back and move forward**.
- **Capabilities**. Specialisation in the law is often encouraged and sometimes rewarded. However, if that means that you have very specific and limited capabilities then that makes you somewhat vulnerable to unexpected change. It is the equivalent to investing all your money in one company's shares. **One of the advantages of diversifying your capabilities as outlined in this book and adopting the T-Shaped Lawyer vision to do different work is that it opens more options for you in the event of a problem arising with your current role**.
- **Purpose.** As I mentioned in the chapter on self -awareness, it is important to try to determine your purpose. **Having a purpose can add meaning to your life and work that provides something to hold onto when the winds of change blow strongly.**
- **Physical and mental health.** You may not be able to control all aspects of your health. However, if you have looked after yourself – your sleep, your diet, physical and mental condition - then that will help you to be able to cope with setbacks.

When setbacks do occur, as they inevitably will, be kind on yourself, do not beat yourself up, and connect with family, friends and in some cases professionals, who can help you get back on your feet.

- **Environment**. Your home, your office, your work colleagues, your friends, and family all make up your environment. Any deficiencies in any aspect of your environment can not only contribute to stress but also reduce your ability to deal with setbacks. **Be mindful of your environment and make any necessary changes before it becomes a problem**.

Focussing on the above, adopting the T-Shaped Lawyer vision and developing yourself along the lines of the T-Shaped Lawyer Framework will make you more resilient just as it enhances your adaptability.Why? Because it will provide you with the confidence that, with broader capabilities and experience, if one door closes another will open for you.

F. <u>Integrity</u>

Last but by no means least, is the quality of integrity or character. Integrity matters for everyone. It is the basis of trust and reputation that individuals and organisations build over time. It only takes one act that lacks integrity to destroy that trust and reputation. After that happens it is extremely difficult, if not impossible, to restore that trust and reputation.

Integrity is especially important for lawyers. In most countries, lawyers have a professional duty to act ethically and with integrity. The other reason why integrity is especially important to you as a lawyer, particularly an in-house lawyer, is that you may be asked to provide ethical guidance to your client. It will be difficult for you to do that with any credibility if you do not act with integrity yourself.

1. What is integrity?

Integrity is the quality of having strong moral principles and consistently adhering to these even in the face of challenges and temptations.

Those principles and values involve a mixture of:

- **External ethical standards** including societal norms, professional obligations such as those referred to above, and ethical guidelines such as those adopted by your organisation and
- **Internal moral values and principles** such as:

- being honest (and rewarding honesty)
- being true to yourself
- being transparent – no hidden agendas
- helping others where you can
- treating others fairly with respect
- showing gratitude
- acknowledging /giving credit to others
- only promise what you are confident you can deliver and deliver on those promises
- being accountable, admit when you make a mistake and when you don't know
- taking responsibility for your actions
- having the courage to speak up when someone else does the wrong thing
- as a leader, encouraging people to speak freely and creating a safe environment for them to do so
- leading by example: *walk the walk don't just talk the talk.*

Integrity is related to, but different from, ethics.

Ethics is the branch of philosophy that provides guidelines and principles for evaluating actions and behaviours based on what is good or bad (values) and what is right or wrong (principles). **Integrity** is the personal characteristic or quality to live up to, and stand up for, these ethical standards.

<u>How to act ethically and with integrity?</u>

Integrity and ethics are vast and complex topics. Fortunately, there are loads of resources[164] available to help you better understand and enhance your integrity. Below are some practical considerations to help you act with integrity.

A helpful place to start might be to inform yourself of your local law society obligations[165] together with the ethical guidelines and values of your organisation. These make up a large part of the extrinsic ethical framework that you need to consider.

Then, if you have not given this topic much thought before, it might be worth thinking about, and documenting, your own values and principles such as those referred to above.

As a lawyer there are two broad situations where your integrity may be tested in practice:

- **in relation to your own actions and decisions and**
- **in relation to the actions and decisions of others including your clients.**

In the first situation you decide what to do. In the second situation the decision is almost always made by your client, and you may have an opportunity, and in some cases an obligation, to offer advice.

In both those situations, the fundamental question that you need to consider is not only what can be done, legally, but what should be done? What is the right thing to do?

Sometimes the answer to that question is obvious, but other times it might be more complex and difficult. How do you answer that question when the answer is not so obvious?

One thing you can do is to consider whether the action in question is contrary to any of the obligations, guidelines, values, and principles referred to above. Taking this step may lead to an obvious answer to the question and provide you with a clear way forward. But what if it is still not clear what should be done in this situation?

The philosophy of ethics can help you to think through what should be done in that situation. Ethics is of course an entire area of study beyond the scope of this book, but there are many resources to help you. For the purposes of this book, it might be worth noting **a few very basic questions that you may wish to consider as a corporate lawyer:**

- **How would I feel about this situation becoming public knowledge tomorrow?**
- **What will this do to my reputation or the reputation of my organisation?**
- **What would happen if everyone did this?**

Some of the most blatant examples of where corporate lawyers have not done the right thing involve situations where they either failed to consider these questions or decided to proceed notwithstanding obvious issues here.

Finally, in difficult situations, do not feel like you need to make the call yourself. **There are a variety of people you could consult for their opinion before deciding what to do or how to advise a client.**

Examples:

- Your legal colleague or your manager are obvious contacts unless they are involved in the situation.
- If they are involved, then there is your human resource contact, or possibly your manager's manager in an extreme case.
- In some countries it is also possible to contact external ethics counsellors for advice.

One specific difficult situation in a work context is when someone you work with has acted, or is proposing to act, unethically. What should you do in this situation?

Whilst it is simple to say that you should always act with integrity, there is no simple answer to this question because each situation is unique. That said, below are a few general comments worth considering:

- If the action does not raise any legal issues and does not violate any aspect of the extrinsic framework referred to above, then your choice of whether to do something, and if so what to do, will depend on the extent to which it falls short of your own values and principles.

- If the action does raise a legal issue and/or could amount to a breach of the extrinsic ethical framework, then:

    - To the extent that it is only a proposed action you should directly or indirectly exert your influence so that any action taken is legal and ethical.
    - If the action has happened already then you should apply your risk assessment skills as explained earlier in the book. You should consider and follow any applicable corporate and/or professional guidelines on reporting and how to deal with the situation. You also need to consider whether an internal investigation is appropriate and, in some cases, whether external reporting to a regulator, or communications to affected parties, is necessary or appropriate.

- Remember your client is the company not individual executives. That has at least two implications:

    - If the interests of the company diverge with those of the executive that you are advising, then you need to inform the executive to obtain independent legal advice.
    - It is difficult to imagine a situation where the long-term interests of a company – as opposed to the short-term interests of some executives – would ever favour some illegal or unethical actions. That should give you the confidence to call out such actions, no matter how difficult it might be to do so, and to find alternative ways to achieve the objectives.

- You need to be mindful of document retention policies and take steps to avoid document destruction in anticipation of legal proceedings.
- **At risk of stating the obvious, in no circumstances should you participate, or even acquiesce, in any cover up of an illegal or unethical act.**

Dealing with such a situation, especially as an in-house lawyer is never easy. **Does being a T-Shaped Lawyer help or exacerbate the situation?**

As I mentioned in the discussion on business partnering, some people might say that you risk compromising your integrity if you become a businessperson and provide business advice and do business work.

In my experience, working as a T-Shaped Lawyer for over a quarter of a century around the world, I can say that I never had to compromise my integrity. The alternative of minimising your exposure to the business and sticking to just legal advice may be 'safer' but your integrity is your 'safety net' that allows you to fully embrace the T-Shaped Lawyer vision.

Also, being a T-Shaped Lawyer means that you will have opportunities, that you would not otherwise have as an i-shaped lawyer, to add significant value to the company by influencing business colleagues to act legally and ethically before actions/decisions are taken.

As mentioned at the beginning of this chapter, all the qualities identified in the Framework are desirable and all are helpful, if not essential, for a successful and fulfilling personal and well as professional life. These human qualities are going to be increasingly more important as we focus in on what distinguishes us as humans from increasingly capable machines and how we can best work together with these technologies[166].

That said, it is not necessarily appropriate for everyone to try to develop all these qualities all at once. Rather, a more pragmatic approach may be to gain an understanding of the extent to which you possess these qualities. You can do that through self-assessments and/or by obtaining feedback from those who you trust.

To the extent that you may be deficient in one of these qualities – especially if that deficiency is creating problems for you – then you might want to focus on developing that quality.

CHAPTER 7

T-SHAPED LAWYER MINDSETS

As we discussed in Chapter 1, understanding your current mindsets is a critical part of becoming more self-aware. But there are three specific mindsets that are key components of the T-Shaped Lawyer Framework to become a T-Shaped Lawyer.

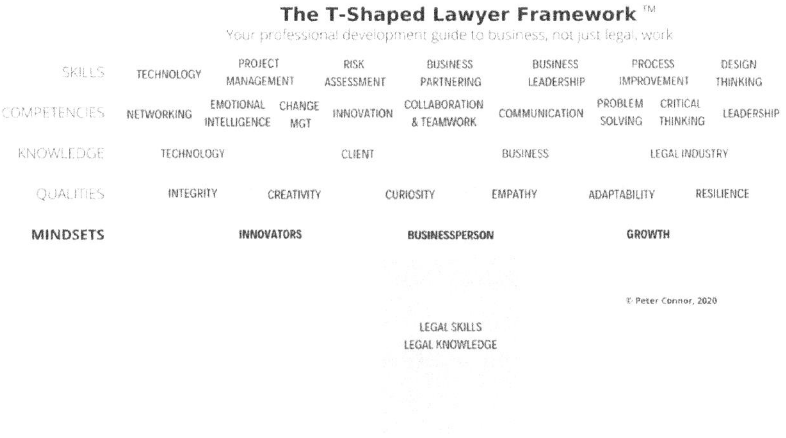

Before I explain those mindsets, it is worthwhile to provide a brief general overview of the basics of mindsets.

A. <u>The Basics of Mindsets</u>

What are mindsets and why are they important?

Mindsets are like implicit theories or personal paradigms. They are assumptions or beliefs that are not necessarily conscious, but that impact how we think and behave, make decisions, and form preferences. They have been compared to a computer operating system; invisible, but critical to how the computer works and the results it produces.

Because mindsets are like filters in your brain, you need to know whether they are blocking or facilitating your thinking and your behaviour required to achieve your aspirations and vision. To put it another way, **mindsets are** what the eminent psychologist, Professor Carol Dweck, refers to as ***'the psychological foundation for upskilling and for success'***.

For that reason, I place mindsets at the base of the dimensions of the T-Shaped Lawyer Framework. Mindsets are not of themselves sufficient. However, if you ignore mindsets, then there may be little point in trying to develop new skills and competencies.

How do you know what mindsets you currently have?

As mentioned in Chapter 1, there are assessments available for most of the major mindsets. It is important to do these assessments because often people believe that they have a particular mindset, but the results of an objective assessment suggest otherwise.

Can you change your mindset and if so, how?

Mindsets are just beliefs in your mind, and you can change your mind. Neuroscience shows us that our brains continue to develop and change even as adults. The brain can be reshaped over time, forming new neural pathways. Neuroscientists call this tendency *neuroplasticity.* These neural pathways are developed by doing or thinking specific things. The things that we do or say more often become hard-wired into our brains as habits. These habits form defined 'routes' in our brain, which become easier to use over time.

Carol Dweck has conducted extensive studies into mindsets over many years and she '*has found that mindset can be changed, and that significant changes in attitudes and behaviours can occur as a result. In other words, our mindset is discretionary. It's something we have the power to revise if we want to—when we become aware of what our mindset is.*[167]'

You can change your mindsets through what are known as **interventions**. One type of intervention that I use in my workshops is to role play the different mindsets in different scenarios. By putting yourself in and out of a particular mindset, you can soon catch yourself when you slip into a one mindset, and you can then consciously change to another mindset.

Another intervention involves the concept of **unlearning**. Often, to move forward in a new direction, you need to first take a few steps back. Unlearning is not about forgetting what you know. Rather it is about consciously discarding one mindset and choosing the new mindset.

<u>What are the key mindsets required to become a T-Shaped Lawyer?</u>

Of all the many different possible mindsets[168] there are three specific mindsets that are critical to become a T-Shaped Lawyer and to do business work not just legal work.

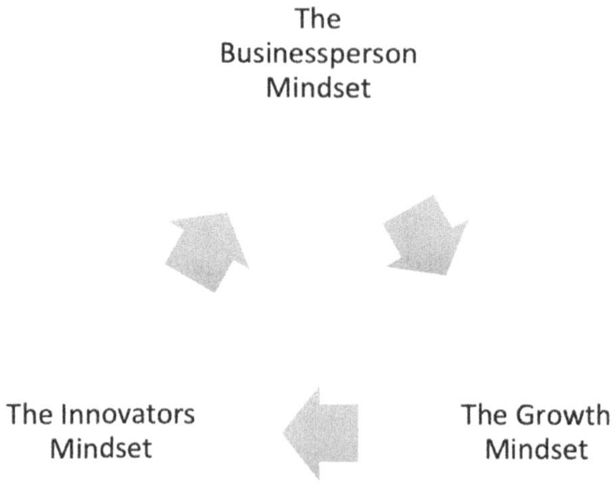

I have selected these three specific mindsets for the Framework because:

- **The Growth Mindset** is essential to believing that you can change yourself in general.
- **The Businessperson Mindset** is essential to believing that you can change yourself in a very specific way that is critical to become a T-Shaped Lawyer.
- **The Innovators Mindset** is essential to believing that you can effect significant change in your work.

B. **The Businessperson Mindset**

The first, and most important mindset for the purpose of becoming a T-Shaped Lawyer, is what I call the ***Businessperson Mindset™.*** I explain in detail what I mean by this mindset, and how to develop it, in Chapter 4 of my first book. It is crucial, without which it is almost impossible to become a T-Shaped Lawyer.

To briefly summarise, a Businessperson Mindset, is in contrast with a 'Just A Lawyer Mindset'. **It involves you thinking of yourself as a businessperson and thinking like a businessperson**. Having this mindset goes above and beyond being business minded. You can be business minded but still think of yourself as a lawyer first and foremost, and still not think like a businessperson as I explain in the first book.

C. **The Growth Mindset**

The second T-Shaped Lawyer Mindset is the Growth Mindset.

Trying to develop new skills and competencies may be a futile exercise if you have what Carol Dweck[169] refers to as a *fixed mindset*. According to Dweck, if you do not have a *growth mindset* you are not ready to change. You will not have the psychological foundations that underpin a belief that you can be competent at something like learning new skills and competencies to work in completely new ways.

If you have a fixed mindset, you believe that you are born with a certain level of intelligence, abilities, personality, or competencies and that these cannot be changed in any significant way. You are primarily concerned about looking smart or not looking silly. As a result, you tend to avoid new challenges and risks, give up when something becomes difficult, view setbacks as failure, are not willing to put in effort to overcome obstacles, dismiss criticism and feel threatened by the success of others. Some of these comments apply to many lawyers that I have met over the years.

By contrast, **if you have a growth mindset,** you understand that you may start with a certain intelligence, personality and set of abilities and competencies but that you can fundamentally change all of these through learning and effort. You have a strong desire to learn and develop yourself. As a result, you tend to seek out and thrive in new challenges, be willing to put in effort, persevere in the face of setbacks, see failures as a chance to learn and do better next time, welcome feedback and find inspiration and lessons in the success of others.

If you do a growth mindset assessment[170], bear in mind that it may be that you have a growth mindset in some areas, for example sport or music, and yet have a fixed mindset in other areas, for example art. Obviously the important area for the purposes of this book is your work and how you think of yourself and your capabilities to do new business work.

The key feature of a growth mindset is a yearn to learn. Curiosity and lifelong learning become a priority for someone with a growth mindset and that is becoming increasingly important. As the World Economic Forum report on the Future of Jobs stated:

'a mindset of agile learning will be needed on the part of workers as they shift from the routines and limits of today's jobs to new, previously unimagined futures'[171].

What are some obstacles for lawyers adopting a growth mindset?

One problem I encounter frequently is that many lawyers do not place sufficient value on continued learning, training, and development. They believe that their education is finished once they complete school and university studies and that it is now all about gaining more legal work experience. They will do training but only the bare minimum necessary to satisfy any continuous professional development (CPD) requirements that my apply. It becomes a tick the box compliance exercise. If you are reading this book, then chances are that you are not one of those lawyers. More likely, you are someone who appreciates the crucial importance of lifelong learning and having a constant and insatiable curiosity.

A related problem is the fact that most lawyers are extremely busy. As a result, reading, training and development, become optional activities that, often, are deferred until 'later'. Dominic Price, the Future of Work director at Atlassian, says:

'training may seem like a tax on today's productivity, but it is actually an investment in tomorrow's productivity'.

Creating time to learn and develop is one of the many critical things you need to find time to do, over and above handling urgent daily tasks.

Finally, many lawyers pride themselves on being right, sounding smart, impressing others, and knowing everything. That sort of perspective is not conducive to adopting a growth mindset. As Satya Nadella, the Microsoft CEO, says **'you want to be a *learn-it-all* not a *know-it-all*'**!

D. The Innovators Mindset

The third T-Shaped Lawyer Mindset is the Innovators Mindset.

As highlighted in Chapter 1 of the first book, in a constantly and rapidly changing world, individuals, teams, and organisations are making constant changes to cope and prosper. Innovation is, therefore, now a top priority for every organisation, department, and firm. What does that mean for you?

You could try to ignore innovation, leave it up to others and focus instead on just getting your daily tasks completed. Alternatively, you could look for ways that you could contribute to innovation [172] and, if you do, you are likely to be valued more by your organisation or firm.

Innovation is a widely misunderstood term, largely because it has been misused to describe changes irrespective of whether they truly qualify as innovation or not. A detailed discussion on the proper meaning of innovation and what is means for legal departments and firms is beyond the scope of this book.

However, I have provided a perspective on my view on the meaning of innovation in Chapter 4 on the innovation competency.

For a specific focus on the innovation mindset, I am going to refer to the research and work of Dennis Stauffer. I do not necessarily agree with everything he has to say about innovation, but his work on the innovation mindset is unique and instructive.

His research establishes that it is difficult, if not impossible, for you to contribute effectively to innovation if you do not have what he calls an *innovation mindset*. However, he also concludes, citing Carol Dweck, that it is possible to change your current mindset to adopt an innovation mindset through interventions. To do that you need to first understand your current mindset[173].

What does having an innovators mindset mean?

There is a lot of theory behind Stauffer's innovation mindset concept, and I have included in the notes references for those who would like to read and understand this theory[174]. However, for the purposes of this book, a simple way to understand what Stauffer means by the *innovation mindset* (IM) is to contrast it with what he calls a *status quo mindset* (SQM).

He breaks down the innovation process down into four stages, focussing on beliefs, values, and behaviours, and highlights the differences at each stage between the two mindsets. The table below provides an insight into the contrasting mindsets.

Contrast between Innovation and Status Quo Mindset

Phases	What	IM would	SQM would
Idea Phase	Ideas and new possibilities are generated	Use imagination, welcome novel ideas, and actively consider new possibilities	Prefer what they already know, be sceptical of new possibilities and less interested in novelty
Action Phase	Some ideas are actioned	Want to try new things, explore, and experiment	Prefer to apply existing knowledge and procedures
Reality Phase	Involves observing how an idea works in practice	Be open to negative and positive results and keen to ascertain accurate data	Look for validation and assurance that the idea did work
Feedback Phase	The data received from the reality phase is assessed	Be keen to discover and will be slow to draw conclusions preferring to explore multiple alternatives	Tend to interpret data to confirm their preconceived idea

Source: Dennis Stauffer

What are some obstacles for lawyers adopting an innovators mindset?

Being risk averse, a common trait for lawyers, could become an obstacle to adopting an innovators mindset. Many lawyers are hardwired to look for problems with any idea. Having an innovation mindset involves embracing a **'what if'**, rather than a **'why not'**, attitude.

Likewise, it will not help if you are a perfectionist, hate to fail or are unwilling to try something that is not certain to succeed. To have an innovator's mindset involves being willing to open your mind to new possibilities, experiment and fail, learn from the attempt, refine your approach, and try again even if others are not supportive.

If you do not have an innovators mindset, using interventions like those mentioned earlier in the chapter can help you to change your mindset to adopt one. An innovators mindset is important to becoming a T-Shaped Lawyer because:

- transforming yourself into a T-Shaped Lawyer, and fundamentally changing your work, is the ultimate innovation project!
- that mindset will help you to innovate by identifying and actioning opportunities to do business work utilising the other components of the T-Shaped Lawyer Framework.

Although this chapter on mindsets is at the end of the book, in practice, mindsets should be one of the first components that you focus on as explained in the next chapter on how to apply the Framework.

CHAPTER 8
HOW TO USE THE T-SHAPED LAWYER FRAMEWORK

The T-Shaped Lawyer Framework can be used by individual lawyers as a guidebook for your professional development. It can also be used by firms and legal departments as the basis of your professional development and training programs for the department or firm, and for so much more.

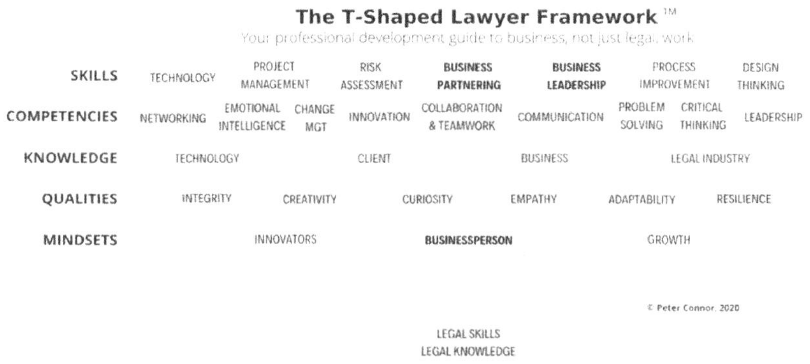

This chapter will explain how to use the Framework in practice by answering some typical questions.

A. <u>Using the Framework as individual lawyers</u>

i. When should I start using the Framework?

As I highlighted in the first book, the time to start doing client business work is now. There is no need to wait to start providing business advice or looking for business leadership opportunities simply because you feel that you might be deficient in any one or more components of the Framework.

That said, if you are going to increasingly do more client business work and to support internal business work you want to be better at doing it. **Developing and using the Framework capabilities is how you can become a better, more mature T-Shaped Lawyer.**

I have met only a handful of fully mature T-Shaped Lawyers as shown on the T-Shaped Lawyer Spectrum[175]. In most cases, it will take quite a lot of time to get to that level and it will involve a transformation, not a mere improvement. **That means the sooner you start the lifelong journey to becoming a mature T-Shaped Lawyer, the better. That is why you should start using the Framework now!**

ii. How should I start to use the Framework and this book?

If you think of it as heading out on a journey to a new and different destination – to be a T-Shaped Lawyer – then think of the T-Shaped Lawyer Framework as your map and this book as your Lonely Planet-type travel companion guidebook for your journey.

Like such a travel guide, ideally you would start by quickly skimming through this book. The reason to do that is to gain an overview of what you will need for the journey ahead. At this stage it is not necessary to understand and remember everything, nor to plan your journey in detail.

iii. How should I plan the first part of my professional development journey? Which components should I focus on?

When it comes time to plan the first part of your journey, then a good place to start is to ascertain the delta between what you need for the journey and what you have currently. This assessment process, that I have mentioned in various parts of the book, will then inform some obvious areas of development for you to focus on initially.

You can self-assess but it is also worthwhile to ask your manager, or others that know you, to provide their assessment. Ideally this assessment process should be undertaken at least once a year. The outcome of these assessments will provide one significant data point to help you plan your professional development journey.

When you are planning the initial part of your journey it is also important to remember the distinction between the different horizontal dimensions of the Framework. Bearing this in mind has the following general implications for applying it in practice:

- **The mindsets are something you can and should work on right from the outset**. Without these it will be difficult to make much progress, and time spent on developing other components may not help you as much. You should continue to work on the Framework mindsets unless and until you feel you have fully adopted them.

- **The qualities and knowledge dimensions are something to be conscious of, and to work on, continually over time**. There is usually no urgency in relation to any of these components unless a deficiency in any one component is causing you problems in which case you might focus on that area.
- **There is also typically no rush to develop the competencies**, but you will often experience a significant return on your efforts to develop these and they can be used in a wide range of situations.
- **The skills are something that, in general, are worth developing, at least to a basic level, as soon as possible**. The reason for that is because they will allow you to make an immediate impact with your work. Each skill is relevant in slightly different ways.

Examples:

- **Business partnering** is not only a skill but a fundamental aspect of being a T-Shaped Lawyer because it involves providing business input and advice. This skill is something that, right from the outset, every lawyer should focus on enhancing and doing more regularly.
- **Business leadership** is also a fundamental aspect of being a T-Shaped Lawyer because it involves doing business work. However, opportunities to show business leadership do not come along every day and so the key here is to be able to identify such an opportunity when it does arise and then know what to

do in that situation. That said, business leadership is a crucial skill because it personifies what you should be aspiring to spend a considerable amount of time doing in the future.

- **Risk assessment** is something you currently do quite frequently. You can achieve an immediate impact if you can advise on risk as suggested in the book. It should not take long to learn how to do that. It is just a matter of doing it every time you engage in risk assessment.
- There are a wide variety of **data and digital skills**. Some you will already have. Some you will need as soon as possible. Others can be developed over time as the need arises.
- **Process improvement and project management** are skills that should not take that long to understand at least at a basic level. Learning these to a basic level, as soon as possible, will allow you to identify when this skill set is required in a particular situation so that you can enlist experts in these areas to assist. You can learn these in more detail over time as you get involved in work that involves these skills.
- **Design Thinking,** unlike legal design, is a skill that you may not use that frequently, at least initially. However, it is worth understanding this skill as soon as possible at least to a basic level. That is because it shows you how to see things from the perspective of your client. Also, when opportunities do arise to use design thinking it can lead to breakthrough innovative outcomes.

Planning the initial part of your professional development journey is a bit like planning a travel journey. The background comments above, and the assessments, will inform some obvious places to focus on initially. However, just like with any trip, it is likely that you will stumble upon a situation which justifies changing the initial plan. Spontaneously diving a bit deeper into a particular skill, competency, or knowledge area, especially if it arises because of a real-life situation, can provide some of the very best development and learning opportunities.

iv. How can you learn about the component areas of the Framework?

This crucial question raises many important and interesting sub-questions such as:

- *where and when can you source the information you need to learn?*
- *how do you decide what level of understanding you need and how much time to devote to something?*
- *what process should you follow to learn? how do you learn?*

This book will provide you with a useful starting point so that you have at least a basic understanding of the relevant mindsets, skills, competencies, qualities, and areas of knowledge to help you become a T-Shaped Lawyer. However, to enhance your development beyond this basic level there are various other mixed-modal possible sources including the following:

Cohort courses such as the T-Shaped Lawyer courses	Training courses from your company, firm or third parties
MOOCs such as Udacity, Coursera, edX, LinkedIn Learning often free	Social media platforms such as LinkedIn to follow thought leaders
Podcasts from thought leaders	Attending in-person and virtual conferences and webinars
Mentoring or coaching	Observing others at work
Leverage job aids such as precedents and playbooks	Reading books and articles

The good news is that there are now so many different sources of learning. The challenge is to select the ones that will most help you achieve your objectives with minimal bias and maximum return for your valuable time.

Adding a social element to your learning can make it more fun and is often also associated with opportunities to network. However, be careful to check how you are spending your time and that you really are benefiting and learning from the time you are devoting to each learning source.

Speaking of time, it is important to create time to learn. Sometimes learning can be 'squeezed' into small pockets of time for example travelling to and from work. However, some topics, require you to focus, reflect and devote larger chunks of time uninterrupted by calls, emails, and social media communications. There are many resources[176] to help you create and manage your time to learn in these different ways.

Increasingly, as organisations focus more on learning and skills development, the question of ***'how do you learn'*** will become one that you need to be able to answer. One of the many advantages of the Framework is that it provides you with a ready-made and convincing answer to that question. In other words, you can say that you use the Framework to inform your learning and professional development and substantiate that with assessments and evidence of what you have learned and how you have used it in your work.

v. Is there more to the Framework than just learning about the component areas?

Continual lifelong learning is extremely important as explained further in the next chapter. However, the point of learning is not just for academic purposes. In other words, the idea is not just to learn for learning sake.

Learning the skills and competencies in the Framework is so that you can use them not just in your traditional legal work but, crucially, also in business advice and business work. **To connect your learning to a specific purpose, an underlying transformation in your work, lies at the heart of the theory of transformative learning as mentioned earlier in the book**. In other words, this maximises the chances of the learning being effective for adults.

Ultimately, the best way to learn is to do. No amount of reading about golf will help your golf game. To achieve that you need to practise new skills and then try to use these in a game of golf on the course.

vi. How can you practice the Framework skills and competencies?

One way to practice is to set up exercises or simulations with members of your department or firm or to bring in an external facilitator to help you do that. Alternatively, look out for opportunities to participate in a training session with others in your organisation. Third parties also offer sessions on some of the Framework skills and competencies.

Whichever way you choose to practise, try to adopt the notion of *deliberate practice*[177] which is the process of working in a specific, purposeful, and strategic way to improve any skill or competence.

Ultimately the best way to practice and develop the Framework skills and competencies is to use them in your work. That is precisely how I discovered and developed them when I worked as a lawyer. **This type of learning is referred to as direct or active learning.**

vii. How can you use the Framework skills and competencies?

Except for business partnering and business leadership, most of the Framework skills and competencies are used by an ever-increasing number of people in the corporate legal industry. However, almost without exception, they use these skills and competencies to do internal business work or, to a lesser extent, in relation to their legal work. It is worthwhile to use them for this purpose and you should also look to use them in that way.

However, if there is only one point you remember about this book, it is that you can, and should, also use these skills and competencies to do client business work. In other words, to provide business advice and do business leadership work where the primary beneficiary is the client's business and not the legal department or firm. Not many people use the skills and competencies in this way. If you do, then this is how you can add substantially more value for your clients and how you can become a T-Shaped Lawyer.

How can you use the skills and competencies in this new and different way? As I explained earlier in this chapter, each skill and competency are different. Some skills and competencies, such as business partnering, risk assessment, networking, and communication, can be used by every lawyer immediately as explained in the earlier discussion on these areas. Others, such as business leadership, change management, design thinking, process improvement and project management, require you to look out for opportunities to initiate or participate in projects or other initiatives.

Clearly, it will be easier for in-house lawyers to identify such opportunities to use these skills and competencies to do business work for the benefit of the business. However, as I explained in the discussions on business partnering and business leadership, there is still substantial scope for lawyers, and other professionals, working in firms to use the skills and competencies in this way.

In summary, every individual you should prepare a Professional Development Plan. The Framework, together with the legal skills and knowledge dimension, can provide the basis for that plan. The plan should state, at a minimum:

- what general areas of the Framework you plan to focus on
- what specific learning activities you intend to undertake

- when you plan to do that
- how you plan to fund those activities, and
- how you plan to use what you have learned.

The plan should be shared with your manager - who can provide input and perhaps a funding contribution - updated on a regular basis, and you should keep a copy of it as evidence of your learning credentials.

B. <u>Using the Framework as individual who are not lawyers</u>

For those of you who work in legal departments and firms in a capacity other than as a lawyer the Framework can be used just as effectively. Most of the general comments made in this chapter above apply equally to you.

That said there are some differences as I shall explain below.

Of course, the most fundamental difference is that you are not providing legal advice to your clients and most of you will have limited interactions with business clients. As a result:

- the vertical 'legal' dimension of the Framework would be replaced with whatever area of expertise you specialise in if any.
- most of you will be engaged in internal business work and so the T-Shaped skills are extremely relevant but mostly when we add the prefix 'legal' to them as explained in that chapter. The one exception would be risk assessment where you would apply this skill in relation to internal business work.

- that said, you should also be on the lookout for opportunities to engage in business leadership and, in these cases, the skills without the 'legal' prefix would be applicable.
- it is unlikely that you will have the opportunity to engage in business partnering and so this is not a focus area for you.
- all other dimensions and components of the Framework will be applicable to you although you will need to adapt the comments in the book to your work and role.

C. Using the Framework as Leaders of Legal Departments and Firms

While individuals can apply the Framework as mentioned above, leaders of legal departments and firms can also leverage the framework in a slightly different way.

Firms and legal departments can, as my clients do, use it for a variety of purposes such as:

- in the hiring process to look for capabilities and a willingness to learn and change and not just years of post-qualification experience.
- as part of assessments, performance reviews, recognition, rewards, and professional development planning.
- to inform training programs for the department or firm.
- by appointing champions to develop deeper expertise in the Framework component areas.
- to attract, retain and develop top talent. Nothing is more impressive than being able to say how you use the Framework to show that you take professional development seriously and

that those in the firm or department will constantly learn, grow, and be recognised as such.

If leaders of firms and legal departments want their lawyers to become T- Shaped Lawyers then it is essential that, among many other things, they use the Framework in these ways. To use the Framework in these ways, especially for that purpose, will require these leaders to show *adaptive leadership*.[178]

Make no mistake about it, using the Framework skills and competencies to provide business advice and do business work requires an adaptive, not a technical, change for every lawyer. That is important to understand for individuals and for leaders of firms and legal departments because **adaptive change:**

- **is harder to define**. The T-Shaped Lawyer vision outlined in the first book provides such a definition.
- **requires changes in individual attitudes, beliefs, and behaviours.** The Framework mindsets play an important part here.
- **takes more time than a technical change.** This why it is important to start now.
- **will meet with more resistance from some individuals**. Change management becomes crucial to address this factor.
- **delivers more long-term substantial outcomes than a technical change**. This is why it is worthwhile to put in the effort and time to make the changes.

As was noted above, you can use the Framework skills and competencies[179] to help your lawyers provide better legal advice, do better legal work, and support internal business work. For the most part that would involve technical changes because the changes are easier to define, can be made relatively quickly by leadership edict, do not involve a change in belief, and will not necessarily result in long term outcomes that clients will notice or find significantly more valuable.

However, I encourage you to use the Framework for the purpose of helping the lawyers to transform so that they can do client business work and realise the T-Shaped Lawyer vision. The promise of substantially more long-term outcomes that provide more value for your clients, and better prepares lawyers for the future, justifies the greater time and effort required to achieve such an adaptive change.

I encourage, and help, my clients to develop a People Plan. If you are seeking to help your lawyers to become T-Shaped Lawyers, then **that plan amounts to a human transformation plan and not just a traditional professional development program**. The plan needs to incorporate, at the very least, the points identified above.

CONCLUSION

The book has covered a lot of material, and it may help to summarise the key points from the earlier chapters in this book as follows:

- It is universally accepted that lawyers now need a lot more than legal skills and legal knowledge to be successful as a corporate lawyer. Now the question that everyone is grappling with is *what non-legal capabilities do you need?*
- You cannot really answer that question unless and until you answer another intermediate question that virtually no-one is asking - *what will you use these non-legal capabilities for? Is it for legal work?*
- It should be obvious that non-legal skills are primarily to do **non-legal work.**
- Non-legal skills and other non-legal capabilities can help you to do or support **internal business work**.
- They are critical for you to be a T-Shaped Lawyer – a businessperson, not just a lawyer, who provides business input/advice, not just legal advice, and does business work, not just legal work for the benefit of the business of clients (**client business work**).
- No one skill or set of skills will suffice. **You will need a combination of skills, competencies, mindsets, qualities, and knowledge**. The distinction between these categories is important because of the different way in which you will develop and use them.

- This combination of different areas should ideally be organised in a framework that is designed specifically to achieve your objective for change and helps you to apply a strategic, structured approach to your professional development and your work. As such a framework can provide a frame of reference that, according to Transformative Learning principles, makes learning effective for adults and not some futile exercise.
- **The T-Shaped Lawyer Framework is such a framework. It is specifically designed to help you to be a T-Shaped Lawyer to do not just legal work, but to do or support internal business work and, crucially, to do client business work.**
- Each of the component areas are explained to provide you with a basic level of understanding about what they are, how to develop them and how they can be used to do business, not just legal, work.
- This book will not make you an expert in any one area but remember the The-Shaped Lawyer is a Legal Expert Business Generalist. Your aim, at least initially, is to understand each area only to the extent necessary to identify when a different skill set may be required and, at least, be able to bring in an expert when needed. Over time, you will develop more capability and therefore be able to contribute more to this business work.
- Use the book, and the Framework, as you would a travel companion guide for a journey to a new destination. Flick through it quickly at the start of your journey to becoming a T-Shaped Lawyer. The book explains which areas require closer attention right from the outset. For everything else, dive into the area a bit deeper as your interest or your work dictates

over time. Remember it is a journey and the book and the Framework can help guide you along the way.

- The Framework can be used, and adapted, even if you do not want to be a T-Shaped Lawyer and do not want to business work. It is certainly better than selecting a random set of 'soft' skills to learn.

For some individuals, training and professional development are tick the box exercises to satisfy continuing education requirements to allow you to continue your work as a lawyer. For some leaders of firms and legal departments, training and professional development is something that is allocated a tiny percentage of the overall budget and which, in difficult times, is the first to be cut.

If you are reading this book, then you are probably not like that. Hopefully, especially after reading this book:

- as individual lawyers you:

    - think of yourself as *an economic asset* – 'a bundle of skills and capabilities, not just a role or profession[180]' – that will depreciate in value unless you continue to invest in enhancing and broadening your skills, knowledge and other capabilities through professional development.
    - realise that training, and other forms of professional development, are critical not only to enhance and broaden your skills and capabilities - *your economic inputs* - but also to enhance and broaden your work

    from traditional legal work to also include business work - *your economic outputs.*
  - understand that, with the relentless advance of generative AI and other technologies encroaching on your traditional work, the need to broaden your capabilities and your work as explained in this book is more necessary and urgent than ever before.

- as leaders of firms and legal departments you:

  - think that your lawyers, and your other staff, are your most important asset and that investing in their professional development is not only good for them but also very good for the performance of the firm or department.
  - realise that the reason that the right kind of professional development enhances performance is because it is how your lawyers and other staff can adapt and change their work to add more value for your clients.
  - understand that the Framework provides you with the best way to discharge one of your most fundamental responsibilities as a leader to prepare your team for the future.

Recognising the crucial link between professional development and the greater impact that you can achieve from doing different work, elevates the importance of professional development to a whole new level. As an individual, professional development should become something you find money and time to do regularly and not something that you try to squeeze in 'if and when' you have some spare time. As a leader of a firm or legal department, professional development should be something which is a priority in your budget and is allocated a substantial amount of time, money, and human resources.

In fact, I encourage individual lawyers and leaders of legal departments and firms to take professional development to an even higher level again. The way to do that is to **shift the frame of reference from professional development to continual learning and experimentation in your work.**

Making learning front and centre can become your personal strategy as individuals and a key component of a department or firm's strategy and culture. It can literally change everything.

For individuals, lifelong learning and work experimentation can be how you can reinvent yourself from being just a lawyer to a T-Shaped Lawyer or to some other role. It can be how you prepare yourself for a future where:

- much of the work you currently do is done by technology,
- skills replace jobs as the basis of matching you with work[181],
- *'how do you learn?'* and *'show me your skills credentials'* become the key questions asked in job interviews.

As Peter Senge said: *'the rate at which you can learn and adapt may well be the only sustainable competitive advantage[182]'*

Also, as the authors of the Adaptation Advantage state:

'a single dose of education - a process that infers an end state of being educated – isn't sufficient... Instead, we need to swap education for learning, a continuous state of discovery and reinvention. Work, then, leverages that learning and the work itself becomes another form of learning.[183]'

My primary aim in writing this book, together with the first book, is to challenge your thinking as individual lawyers about what you want from your career, what you can be and do in your work, and how you can change yourself and your work to achieve your objectives. This book can be your guidebook to help you make that journey on your own although I can assist if needed.

Although the books are primarily written for individual lawyers, my secondary aim was to provide leaders of legal departments and firms with enough information to see how the T-Shaped Lawyer Vision and the Framework can be adopted at a legal department and firm level. It should be obvious to such leaders that this extends way beyond professional development and impacts every aspect of the legal department and firm as you can see, for example, from the high-level overview below of the T-Shaped Team Framework™ for legal departments. Explaining this Framework could be an entire book and, for now at least, is something I will reserve for my workshops.

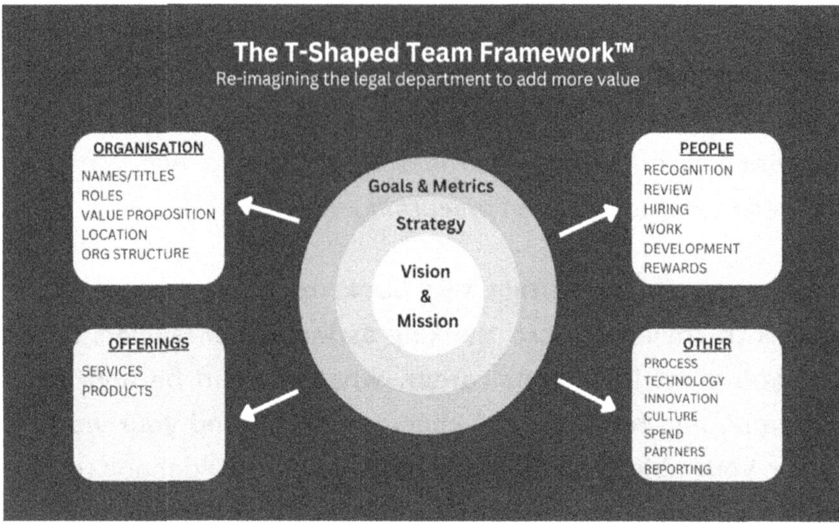

Finally, it is ironic that for a profession that is so precise when it comes to the law itself, how imprecise lawyers often are when discussing change in the practice of law and ways of working.

It is just as important to be precise in the language of change in the practice of law as it is in the language of law. Without this precision it will be difficult, if not impossible, for you to change in any meaningful way. The reason for that is because you may not be changing in the way that you think and your efforts to change may not be realising optimal results. To assist you, the appendix provides a Glossary for Change in the Corporate Legal Industry.

I wish you well in whatever paths you choose to follow and hope that the books provide you some inspiration and guidance. If this book was helpful for you, it would be appreciated if you let others know your thoughts to help spread the word.

APPENDIX

A GLOSSARY FOR CHANGE IN THE CORPORATE LEGAL INDUSTRY

It is crucial to be as precise about the language of change as it is about the language of the law. If not, you may be fooling yourself about change, you are unlikely to achieve your change objectives, and it will frustrate efforts for real change in the corporate legal industry.

This glossary is my contribution to a common language that everyone in the corporate legal industry can use to talk about, and action, change. Undoubtedly there are other terms that could be added to this glossary. However, other than technology specific terms that are covered in various existing glossaries, the terms below are in my experience the ones that matter most. They are also the terms that are most frequently used and misused.

I use these terms, and elaborate on them, in my books – *The T-Shaped Lawyer: A New Vision for You and Your Work* and *The T-Shaped Lawyer Guidebook: A Framework for Your Professional Development.*

Adaptability: the ability to adjust as a result, or in anticipation, of changed circumstances.

Business Development: the creation of value for a business by identifying and executing business enhancement opportunities. Typically associated with law firms but can also be applicable for in-house legal departments.

Business Leadership: a form of client business work that extends beyond the provision of business advice or input and involves a greater commitment of time than business partnering and the ability to influence others.

Businessperson Mindset™: a mindset developed by Peter Connor and defined in *The T-Shaped Lawyer: A New Vision for You and Your Work.* It shows how a lawyer can think of yourself as a businessperson, not just a lawyer, and think like a businessperson.

Business Partner: a status you earn with a client when they see you as someone who understands the business and as someone who can help them in their work. Being a business partner is a necessary but not sufficient condition to engage in the activity of business partnering.

Business Partnering: a form of client business work that involves providing business advice or business input either in conjunction with, or separate to, the provision of legal advice. It involves more than being a business partner.

Business Work: for a corporate lawyer is any work that you do other than legal work.

Change Management: the application of a structured process for helping people to accept, adopt and support change to achieve a desired outcome.

Client Business Work: is business work that is specifically for the benefit of the client. It involves helping clients to solve or prevent business problems and to create or optimise business opportunities.

Collaboration: the ability to work effectively with other people who you may not be team members to achieve desired outcomes in an efficient and harmonious way.

Communication: the ability to understand and share information in a meaningful way.

Competency: an ability that helps you to be successful in a range of tasks and jobs. Behavioural competencies are a key dimension of the T-Shaped Lawyer Framework.

Corporate Legal Industry: that part of the legal industry that focuses on corporations including all stakeholders, such as corporate legal departments, law firms, other legal service and product providers, and all the products and services that these stakeholders offer.

Creativity: the ability to come up with ideas and turn them into reality.

Critical Thinking: the ability to question, analyse, interpret, evaluate, and make a judgement about what you read, hear, say or write.

Culture: in a firm or legal department is the beliefs and behaviours that determine how members of the firm and legal department interact and perform.

Curiosity: the impulse to seek new information and experiences and to explore novel possibilities.

Decision Making: the ability to choose between two or more possible courses of action to achieve optimal outcomes.

Design Thinking: an iterative process involving regular user feedback to quickly solve difficult problems and to rapidly develop products and services that meet user's real, as opposed to perceived, needs.

Digital Transformation: using technologies and data to fundamentally change the ways business gets done and creating completely new ways of doing business.

Efficiency: for corporate lawyers involves doing your work as quickly and as cost effectively as possible.

Effectiveness: for corporate lawyers involves doing the right sort of work that adds the most value for your clients.

Emotional Intelligence: emotional and social capabilities that influence the way we perceive and express ourselves, develop and maintain social relationships, cope with challenges, and use emotional information in an effective and meaningful way.

Empathy: the ability to understand and, in some cases share, the feelings of others.

Expert Generalist: an expression coined by Onit Garnesh, the chairperson of Bain & Co management consultants, to describe a person who is an expert in one area but also a generalist in other areas.

Framework: a specific set of factors that is designed to achieve specific outcomes and to provide a structured means to achieve these outcomes.

Growth Mindset: a specific mindset developed and defined by Carol Dweck to show how your capabilities are not fixed but can be changed.

Human Transformation: transforming, not just improving, what work you do and your capabilities to do new and different work.

Innovation: change that adds value especially for your clients.

Innovation Mindset: a mindset developed and defined by Dennis Stauffer to show how you can effect significant change in your work.

Integrity: the quality of having strong moral principles and consistently adhering to these even in the face of challenges and temptations.

Internal Business Work: for legal departments and firms is any business work that is primarily for the benefit of the department and firm. Often referred to as legal operations in legal departments but also includes people management.

Knowledge: understanding of, or information about, a subject gained through experience or education.

Lawyer: a person who is qualified to practice law.

Leadership: the ability to influence people so that they willingly follow.

Legal Expert Business Generalist: an expression coined by Peter Connor to adapt the Expert Generalist idea to corporate lawyers. It involves corporate lawyers adding a business generalist dimension to their legal specialisation. The T-Shaped Lawyer is a version of Legal Expert Business Generalist.

Legal Design: the application of design thinking principles in the field of law to transform legal products, services, work, systems, business strategies, ecosystems, and user experience.

Legal Innovation: a change that adds value for a legal department or law firm.

Legal Operations: a range of internal business work typically for a legal department and a profession of people qualified to do this work.

Legal Process Improvement: the application of process improvement to legal department or law firm processes.

Legal Project Management: the application of project management to legal matters or to internal business initiatives.

Legal Risk Assessment: the application of risk assessment to legal risks.

LegalTech: technology specifically designed for legal departments and law firms.

Legal Work: work that only a qualified lawyer can do the standard necessary in any situation. NB This is a working definition that is more helpful for lawyers than any definition as a matter of law.

Managed Services: similar to outsourcing except typically more co-design of the solution focusing on process and technology and more ongoing collaboration, visibility, and oversight.

Management: the ability to encourage people to execute the vision, strategies and plans to achieve desired goals and outcomes.

Mindset: a set of beliefs that shape how you perceive and make sense of yourself and the world.

Mission: your purpose or reason for existing.

Networking: the ability to build and maintain a range of relationships with people and to share information with them.

Outsourcing: in the legal industry involves transferring work that has been done in a legal department or a law firm to be done by a third-party provider.

Problem Solving: the ability to remove or overcome barriers to the achievement of a goal or desired outcome.

Process Improvement: the ability to define and streamline a process primarily to make it more efficient.

Productisation: of a service involves converting a service offered by people into a product that can be directly accessed by clients without necessarily involving human intervention.

Project Management: the ability to plan and manage a project to achieve the project objectives within scope, time, and cost constraints.

Quality: a personal attribute that is demonstrated independent of context.

Resilience: the ability to cope with changing circumstances and to 'bounce back' in the face of adversity.

Rightsourcing: the allocation of work to the appropriate internal or external resource.

Risk Assessment: the ability to identify, assess and advise on a range of risks.

Self-awareness: the ability to understanding yourself; your feelings, needs, aspirations, preferences, failings, habits, and everything else that makes you the unique individual that you are.

Skill: in a professional sense means expertise needed to achieve a work outcome in a specific context.

Strategy: initiatives designed to achieve your vision or any other priority.

Teamwork: the ability to work effectively with other members of a team to achieve desired outcomes in an efficient and harmonious way.

Transformation: a change from one thing into something completely different that involves more than a mere improvement.

Trusted Advisor: in a professional context is a person that a client, or someone else, would contact to seek advice or input on a wide range of professional, and sometimes personal, matters not just confined to their professional area of expertise. A 'go to' person.

T-Shaped Lawyer: a businessperson, not just a lawyer, who provides business advice, not just legal advice, and does business work, not just legal work, for the benefit of the client, not just the legal department or firm.

T-Shaped Lawyer Framework™: a specific combination of skills, competencies, qualities, knowledge, and mindsets developed by Peter Connor to help lawyers become T-Shaped Lawyers through a structured approach to their professional development.

Value: something that is perceived as important from the perspective of the beneficiary.

Value Proposition: what you can uniquely offer to your clients.

Values: for a firm or legal department are the beliefs and principles that are important to the way you work and interact with others.

Vision: a picture of what you, as an individual or as a legal department or firm, aspire to be in the future.

Work Rationalisation™: an ongoing process and a tool developed by Peter Connor to help lawyers and other professionals in legal departments decide what work to do and what work not to do.

ABOUT THE AUTHOR

Peter Connor is the Founder & CEO of AlternativelyLegal which he formed in 2015 to help corporate lawyers, in-house legal departments and law firms innovate and transform, not just improve, their work. He does that through a range of unique programs and frameworks that he developed and delivers in workshops, cohort training or consulting engagements including:

- **T-Shaped Lawyer Program™** designed for individual lawyers on how to use the T-Shaped Lawyer Framework™ to enhance their capabilities to become T-Shaped Lawyers so that they can do more meaningful and impactful business work, not just legal work.
- **T-Shaped Team Program™** designed to provide guidance to legal departments on the T-Shaped Team Framework™ and how to utilise it to transform the legal department into a team that provides not only legal services, but also business services and products.
- **T-Shaped Firm Program™** designed to provide guidance to law firms on The T-Shaped Firm Framework™ and how to utilise it to transform the firm into a business that provides a range of business services and products not just legal services.

Peter has conducted over 50 workshops around the world for the legal departments of a range of brand name companies including Google, HSBC, Pfizer, ANT Financial / Alibaba, Porsche, Coca Cola, Bayer, AIA, and ANZ Bank. He has also worked with firms like Baker McKenzie, Minter Ellison, and Rajah & Tann Asia.

In Australia, Peter was retained by KPMG Law to help them conceive, develop, and deliver their New Law / Legal Operations and Transformation Services product and service offerings for in-house legal departments.

Prior to starting AlternativelyLegal, he worked in a business role, as VP Tech Products, managing software development for the Hong Kong-based compliance firm, Red Flag Group.

Peter has had a diverse, global career as a lawyer for over 25 years. He has lived and worked in Silicon Valley California, Switzerland, England, Hong Kong, and Sydney in the following roles:

- European General Counsel and, later, as Head of Global Compliance for Citrix Systems
- APAC General Counsel, Head of Legal Shared Services, European General Counsel and Head of European Government Affairs for Sun Microsystems.
- Senior Associate at Baker McKenzie in Sydney and Hong Kong.

Peter is the recipient of the Citrix Design Thinking Hero Award and the Sun Microsystems CEO Business Leadership Award for his innovative contributions to the business. He is a widely- published author and Legal Business World, and others, have recognised him as a global thought leader. He regularly speaks at legal conferences around the world on innovation and transformation. He can be contacted at peter.connor@alternativelylegal.com or by connecting on LinkedIn.

ENDNOTES

---

[1] *The T-Shaped Lawyer: A New Vision for You and Your Work.* Peter Connor, November 2023. Available on Amazon Kindle as an ebook and paperback and on Apple Books and Kobo as an ebook.

[2] Of course, there are other outcomes that you are seeking from work, but these are the ones that I will focus on for this book.

[3] By fulfilment I mean a feeling of overall happiness and satisfaction and an opportunity to realise your full potential.

[4] See for example https://www.lawcare.org.uk/ , Ian Hickie, *'Lifestyle'* in Tony Foley and Ian Hickie et al (eds), *Being Well in the Law: A Guide for Lawyers,* (The Law Society of New South Wales, 2016) and https://www.lawsociety.com.au/sites/default/files/2018-08/Being%20Well%20in%20the%20Law%20Guide.pdf

[5] See for example, *Emotionally Intelligent Lawyers: How to Navigate the Psychological Implications of Becoming a Lawyer*. Esperanza Franco. Self-published. July 2023.

[6] It is also, of course, important to your personal life as well but this book focusses on your professional life

[7] For example, https://www.amazon.com.au/Self-Awareness-Emotional-Intelligence-Harvard-Business-ebook/dp/B07C33GBTH, https://www.theschooloflife.com/shop/tsol-press-who-am-i-journal/

[8] See for example. https://www.psychologytools.com/self-help/a-guide-to-emotions/ , https://www.6seconds.org/, *The School of Life: An Emotional Education.* Alain de Botton. Penguin 1st edition, 2020.

[9] https://simonsinek.com/find-your-why/

[10] See for example https://hbr.org/2010/07/how-will-you-measure-your-life, https://www.amazon.co.uk/Purpose-Handbook-beginners-guide-figuring-ebook/dp/B09C6DJBPV/ref=sr_1_2?qid=1677606974&refinements=p_27%3AEloise+Skinner&s=books&sr=1-2&asin=B09C6DJBPV&revisionId=b6d6937e&format=1&depth=1

[11] For example, https://www.andyandrews.com/personal-mission-statement/, https://www.astridbaumgardner.com/blog-and-resources/write-a-life-purpose-statement-in-4-steps-for-fulfillment-and-direction/

[12] PERMA is a well-known approach that you may find helpful to 'map your happy' – see https://positivepsychology.com/happiness-wellbeing-coaching-perma/, and ,https://health.arizona.edu/sites/default/files/data/Map%20Your%20Happy%20PERMA%20worksheet.pdf

[13] For example,

http://www.manifestyourpotential.com/self_discovery/5_discover_life_purpose/statement_examples_of_life_purpose.htm
[14] Penguin Putnam Inc, April 5, 2011- see also https://www.danpink.com/books/drive/
[15] https://ir.law.fsu.edu/cgi/viewcontent.cgi?referer=https://www.google.com/&httpsredir=1&article=1093&context=articles
[16] *The Legal Profession in 2024: The Wider View.* Interview in Harvard Law Today with Professor David Wilkins, the Director of the Centre on the Legal Profession at Harvard Law School. February 21,2024. https://hls.harvard.edu/today/the-legal-profession-in-2024-democracy-salary-and-hiring-general-counsels-and-legal-education/
[17] See the marginal returns from business graphic there.
[18] The T-Shaped Lawyer Framework Assessment tool assesses the key mindsets, skills and competencies from the Framework.
[19] https://en.wikipedia.org/wiki/360-degree_feedback
[20] https://www.atlassian.com/blog/teamwork/johari-window
[21] https://www.gallup.com/cliftonstrengths/en/252137/home.aspx
[22] https://www.myersbriggs.org/my-mbti-personality-type/mbti-basics/
[23] https://erep.com/core-values-index/
[24] https://www.viacharacter.org/
[25] https://storefront.mhs.com/collections/eq-i-2-0
[26] See for example The Whole Lawyer and The Delta Model
[27] See for example https://www.weforum.org/reports/the-future-of-jobs-report-2018
https://www.weforum.org/agenda/2016/01/the-10-skills-you-need-to-thrive-in-the-fourth-industrial-revolution/
https://data.nber.org/reporter/2017number4/deming.html
https://hbr.org/2015/08/research-technology-is-only-making-social-skills-more-important and also *Soft Skills for the Effective Lawyer,* Randall Kiser, Cambridge University Press, 2017.
[28] It is ironic for a profession that prides itself on being precise when it comes to the law, how imprecise lawyers are when it comes to their way of working and their professional development. See my article in ACC Docket Magazine August 2023
[29] Understanding non-legal skills may still be beneficial so that you can understand internal business work but they may be less important than some of the competencies and qualities in the Framework.
[30] Originally in 1978 and subsequently refined and developed in various studies, articles and books

[31] Work Rationalisation™ is the name I have given to a process every legal department and firm should do on a regular basis to review their current work and to find ways to do less of certain types of work.

[32] Negotiation is both a legal skill and a non-legal skill because it can be used for legal work but also it can be used for business work. However, because it is something most lawyers are familiar with and/or spend some time on developing I do not cover it specifically in the T-Shaped Lawyer Framework

[33] Legal design can be used to prepare template contracts and policies. Is that legal work or is that internal business work? Likewise, legal project management is used to manage legal work. Does the management of legal work constitute legal work or internal business work? Other than those somewhat 'borderline' situations, most references to these skills with legal as a prefix are clearly to internal business work.

[34] How to become a trusted advisor to some clients is covered in depth in Chapter 5 of my first book.

[35] For example, The ACC CLO Survey 2020 - https://www.acc.com/clo2020 - reveals that legal risk receives far less management attention—15.4%, as a risk category— than business, 63.4%, and financial risk, 23.1% . This means that if you are only focussing on legal risk you are missing a huge opportunity to add value for your clients.

[36] See The Effectiveness Project. https://ltc4.org/effectiveness-project/?fbclid=IwAR3JiEFVEOtfK1FqzTG3SwMiL64yeBn-_amCY_Vnpy-egMKuc12pDb8XkrM

[37] See for example the 2012 American Bar Association Comment 8 to the Model Rule of Professional Conduct 1.1 implemented in most US States.

[38] See for example https://www.wearelegit.ai/ ,https://storage.googleapis.com/msgsndr/ilh4ju1FhQ04qxg0DDIe/media/6487bcce5b1dfe7b38f6e7f5.pdf

[39] Your IT department may be able to help but also see, for example, https://www.wordrake.com/tech-tips?fbclid=IwAR3IPDEMFHgmaDN9V6VUJbKUgAcFu6vDpAKDATYk8GKIzOs7mnIVqllBo9s, https://blog.udemy.com/basic-computer-skills/ and https://www.oneeducation.org.uk/basic-computer-skills/

[40] https://www.legalbusinessworld.com/post/2018/03/31/will-law-firms-become-software-companies

[41] We will discuss the idea of clients in more detail in the section on clients in the knowledge chapter of the book. However, for present purposes, clients refer to legal departments for law firms and to the business of any company for both law firms and legal departments.

[42] The concept of adjacency was explained in the first book. In practice a T-Shaped Lawyer will typically apply technology and use the other non-legal skills in areas of the business that the lawyer is involved in rather than just some random part of the business unrelated to the work of that lawyer.
[43] This an example of productising a service as I mention in the first book.
[44] OUP Oxford, 3rd Edition, February 7, 2023
[45] For example, https://www.browserstack.com/guide/learn-software-development-process
[46] https://www.buyinglegal.com/
[47] Although sometimes confusingly referred to as legal business processes
[48] James P Womack and Daniel T Jones. *Lean Thinking - Banish Waste And Create Wealth In Your Corporation* .Free Press 2nd Edition 2003
[49] https://www.legalbusinessworld.com/single-post/2017/03/08/Lean-Is-The-Path-To-The-Perfect-Legal-Practice-An-Essay-in-Three-Parts and https://agileattorney.com/the-seven-wastes-of-lawyers/
[50] https://www.sixsigmadaily.com/seven-eleven-awarded-lean-six-sigma-legal-department/, https://m.acc.com/valuechallenge/resources/upload/ProcessImprovement-6-16.pdf, https://www.seyfarth.com/images/content/7/5/v1/7598/LITDecJan2014LeanSixSigma.pdf,
[51] *"Process is the Key to Technology Success"* (Technology Industry Services Industry Association)
[52] https://www.acc.com/sites/default/files/2019-04/ProcessImprovement-6-16.pdf, https://checklistlegal.com/2017/11/legal-process-mapping-guide/, https://medium.com/@filestage/the-practical-process-improvement-guide-how-to-improve-your-workflow-b792f53c943a,
[53] Project Management Institute definition.
[54] https://www.iilpm.com/ The International Institute of Legal Project Management is a useful resource to learn more about Legal Project Management. See also https://cloc.org/legal-project-management-guide-tools/ and https://www.acc.com/resource-library/legal-project-management for an explanation of how LPM can be applied in an in-house context.
[55] See https://cloc.org/wp-content/uploads/2022/08/MLM-Matter-Lifecycle-Management-for-Legal-Teams-08-11-22.pdf
[56] https://community.cloc.org/viewdocument/legal-project-management-lpm-for-l, https://www.pmi.org/learning/courses/introduction-to-project-management, https://www.coursera.org/specializations/project-management
[57] *The Legal Design Book, Doing Law in the 21st Century*, Astrid Kohlmeier & Meera Kiemola, 2021

[58] https://www.interaction-design.org/literature/topics/wicked-problems
[59] Outlined in Chapter 7 of my first book.
[60] https://designthinking.ideo.com/, https://dschool.stanford.edu/, https://www.openlawlab.com/ , http://www.lawbydesign.co/en/legal-design/, https://www.interaction-design.org/literature/topics/design-thinking
[61] However technical competencies would be covered in the vertical dimension of the Framework.
[62] Refer to the chapter on the Changing Landscape for Lawyers in my first book.
[63] The Centre for Creative Leadership - https://www.ccl.org/, https://www.coursera.org/collections/management-skills
[64] *Leadership in the New Normal*, Lt Gen Russel Honore, Arcadian House Publishing, 1st Edition, October 2012
[65] The prefix Legal tells us that it is for internal purposes within the legal department or firm, just as that prefix had the same meaning for the skills mentioned in the prior chapter.
[66] *Mark Roellig and David M. Love III, "So You Want to Be a General Counsel? How to Maximize Your Chances," ACC Docket volume 30, issue 1 (January/February 2012): 72-83. Copyright © 2012, the Association of Corporate Counsel.*
[67] *Adaptive Leadership: The Heifetz Collection,* Harvard Business Review Press, September 23, 2014
[68] Ditto
[69] In the rare cases where leaders do not appreciate you assuming additional responsibilities beyond your daily tasks, then you may need to fine tune when and how you do this activity.
[70] Chapter 7 of my first book
[71] *Adaptive Leadership: The Heifetz Collection*, Harvard Business Review Press, September 23, 2014
[72] https://www.prosci.com/resources/articles/definition-of-change-management
[73] https://www.prosci.com/resources/articles/definition-of-change-management
[74] See for example, https://www.prosci.com/solutions/training-programs, https://apmg-international.com/product/change-management, https://change-management-institute.com/, https://change-management-institute.com/cmbok/
[75] https://www.prosci.com/methodology/adkar
[76] https://userguiding.com/blog/lewins-change-model-theory/
[77] https://www.kotterinc.com/methodology/8-steps/
[78] https://strategicmanagementinsight.com/tools/mckinsey-7s-model-

framework/
[79] https://whatfix.com/blog/kubler-ross-change-curve/
[80] *Leading Change.* John Kotter. Harvard Business Review Press. 29 November 2012.
[81] https://change-management-institute.com/ and https://apmg-international.com/product/change-management
[82] Chapter 1 of my first book summarises the key changes that impact lawyers.
[83] https://www3.weforum.org/docs/WEF_Future_of_Jobs_2020.pdf
[84] https://online.hbs.edu/blog/post/sustaining-vs-disruptive-innovation
[85] As suggested and explained in my first book.
[86] https://www.foursightonline.com/
[87] See for example https://www.ideou.com/pages/innovation-resources and https://www.ldilibrary.com/ldi-resources,
[88] See for example, https://www.atlassian.com/blog/teamwork/the-importance-of-teamwork,
https://www2.deloitte.com/us/en/insights/focus/human-capital-trends/2019/team-based-organization.html,
[89] For example, Slack, Microsoft Teams and Office 365, Zoom, Google Docs and Meet.
[90] Example of this is Microsoft Legal's development of a tool called HiveMind that uses tagging to automatically store and retrieve email legal advice provided by the legal department and by their external advisors.
[91] For example, Kanban or visual to-do boards see for example https://files.clio.com/marketo/ebooks/lean-legal-three-techniques-for-the-agile-lawyer.pdf
[92] Co-creation is a special kind of collaboration that involves working with a customer to develop solutions for them.
[93] Hackathons are events involving a diverse mix of individuals who attempt in a compressed period of time to solve problems typically involving the development of technology solutions.
[94] *Pulling Together: 10 Rules for High-Performance Teamwork.* John. J Murphy. Simple Truths May 1, 2016. *Smarter Collaboration: A New Approach to Breaking Down the Barriers and Transforming Work.* Heidi K. Gardner and Ivan A. Matviak. Harvard Business Review Press. March 2023.
[95] https://www.amazon.com.au/Give-Take-Helping-Others-Success/dp/0143124986
[96] https://inhouseconnect.org/
[97] https://www.inhousecommunity.com/
[98] https://inview.lawvu.com/
[99] There is a Premium paid version that does provide additional benefits if you

prefer.
[100] https://www.theforage.com/blog/basics/how-use-linkedin, https://www.dummies.com/article/technology/social-media/linkedin/linkedin-for-dummies-cheat-sheet-207381/,
[101] https://www.skillsyouneed.com/ips/listening-skills.html and https://www.oscartrimboli.com/ and *How to Listen. Discover the hidden key to better communication,* Oscar Trimboli, Page Two, October 11, 2022.
[102] *Plain Language for Lawyers,* 4th Edition, Federation Press, Michele Asprey. *Simply Said. Communicating Better at Work and Beyond.* Wiley Press, Jay Sullivan.
[103] https://www2.deloitte.com/us/en/insights/focus/technology-and-the-future-of-work/what-is-work.html, https://www2.deloitte.com/us/en/insights/focus/technology-and-the-future-of-work/redefining-work-for-new-value-creation.html
[104] *The Legal Profession in 2024: The Wider View.* Interview in Harvard Law Today with Professor David Wilkins, the Director of the Centre on the Legal Profession at Harvard Law School. February 21,2024. https://hls.harvard.edu/today/the-legal-profession-in-2024-democracy-salary-and-hiring-general-counsels-and-legal-education/
[105] https://asq.org/quality-resources/five-whys
[106] https://asq.org/quality-resources/root-cause-analysis
[107] https://fourweekmba.com/catwoe-analysis/
[108] https://asq.org/quality-resources/affinity
[109] https://asq.org/quality-resources/fishbone
[110] https://www.ideou.com/pages/brainstorming
[111] For more on understanding intuition compared with reasoning see *Thinking Fast and Slow,* Daniel Kahneman, Farrar, Strauss and Giroux, 2011. Penguin Press
[112] See for example https://www.mindtools.com/cyz4vzu/decision-making
[113] https://www.mindtools.com/aksic2i/decision-matrix-analysis
[114] https://project-management.com/understanding-responsibility-assignment-matrix-raci-matrix/,
[115] https://www.productplan.com/glossary/daci/
[116] Environment, social and governance (ESG) is an increasingly important dimension for all decisions and one that lawyers are in an ideal position to highlight
[117] https://hbr.org/2007/09/performing-a-project-premortem
[118] *Decision Quality: Value Creation from Better Business Decisions.* Carl Spetzer, Hannah Winter, Jennifer Meyer. Wiley, 1st edition Februart 24, 2016. *Decision Making and Problem Solving.* John Adair. Kogan Page 5th edition, July

3, 2022.

[119] For guidance on how to overcome your biases see Kirkebooen, Geir (2009). *Decision Behaviour - Improving Expert Judgement*, In Knut Fredrik Samset; Kjell J. Sunnevag & Terry Williams (ed.), *Making Essential Choices with Scant Information: Front-end Decision Making in Major Projects*. Palgrave Macmillan. ISBN 9780230205864. Chapter 9. s 169 - 194

[120] Cited in an article by Richard Paul, *The State of Critical Thinking Today*, Chapter 3, New Directions for Community Colleges, no 130 Summer 2005, Wiley Periodicals Inc

[121] Most universities offer critical thinking courses or free resources such as https://www.monash.edu/rlo/research-writing-assignments/critical-thinking. Also see https://www.criticalthinking.org/ and books like *Critical Thinking, Tools for taking charge of your learning and your life.* 4th Edition, Richard Paul and Linda Elder, Rowman & Littlefield Publishers, February 1, 2022 and Critical Thinking and Problem Solving, Jack Wilbur, February 7, 2023. https://www.amazon.com.au/Critical-Thinking-Problem-Solving-Decision-Making/dp/B0BV1F28YQ/ref=cm_cr_arp_d_product_top?ie=UTF8

[122] *Emotional Intelligence: Why it can matter more than IQ*, Daniel Goldman, Bantam Books 1995

[123] Ditto and also see https://hbr.org/2017/02/emotional-intelligence-has-12-elements-which-do-you-need-to-work-on

[124] *Primal Leadership: Unleasing the Power of Emotional Intelligence.* Daniel Goleman, Richard Boyatzis and Annie McKee, Harvard Business Review Press, Illustrated edition August 2013.

[125] See for example *The EQ Edge" Emotional Intelligence and Your Success,* Steven J Stein and Howard E Book, Jossey-Bass, 3rd edition April 26, 2011 and *Emotionally Intelligent Lawyers: How to Navigate the Psychological Implications of Becoming a Lawyer*. Esperanza Franco. Self-published. July 2023.

[126] See for example https://www.ihhp.com/free-eq-quiz/ and https://eiexperience.com/resources/emotional-intelligence-quiz/ , https://greatergood.berkeley.edu/quizzes/ei_quiz

[127] https://www.eiconsortium.org/measures/eci_360.html but also run by other certified assessors

[128] https://www.eiconsortium.org/measures/eqi.html but also run by other certified assessors.

[129] There are also a variety of steps that legal departments and firms can take to help their lawyers enhance these areas of knowledge as I explain in The T-Shaped Team Framework and the T-Shaped Firm Framework.

[130] See for example - https://www.khanacademy.org/economics-finance-domain/macroeconomics/macro-basic-economics-concepts

[131] https://www.khanacademy.org/economics-finance-domain/microeconomics

[132] https://www.khanacademy.org/economics-finance-domain/core-finance

[133] Read your local business newspaper such as the Financial Times or the Wall Street Journal or subscribe to various online business news feeds.

[134] The Economist magazine and in particular see https://www.economist.com/economics-a-to-z/
Complete Business Foundations Guide, https://payhip.com/b/DbvMS
also see https://www.youtube.com/watch?v=6RhnJ1fNIX0 and https://personalmba.com/

[135] Industry Specialization, Patrick McKenna, Legal Business World, https://www.legalbusinessworld.com/_files/ugd/b30d31_b986c477f93f40dc880c81daa244a6b0.pdf

[136] For example see https://www.quantumrun.com/consulting/quantumrun-foresight-platform-ai-trend-curation/

[137] See for example *Handbook of Legal Tech,* Colin Levy, GlobeLawand Practice, August 2023 https://www.legaltechtrends.com/ and https://www.legaltechnologyhub.com/

[138] See for example https://www.techtarget.com/whatis/resources/Tech-Explainers, https://techpolicydesign.au/tech-explainers, https://www.linkedin.com/company/genai-works/

[139] https://www.123test.com/personality-test/ free - also https://www.16personalities.com/free-personality-test, Myer Briggs, Caliper, DISC assessments – dominance, influence, steadiness, compliance- https://www.discprofile.com/what-is-disc/overview/ also free versions https://www.crystalknows.com/personality-test and https://www.123test.com/

[140] SAS Curiosity@Work Report 2021 - https://www.sas.com/content/dam/SAS/documents/corporate-collateral/brochures/en-curiosity-at-work-112457.pdf

[141] https://www.emdgroup.com/company/us/curiosity-full-report-us.pdf

[142] Ditto at page 4 of the Report

[143] See https://www.mindtools.com/a2baqhc/questioning-techniques, https://www.amazon.com/Ask-Better-Questions-questions-improve/dp/B085K12HCY

[144] *World Economic Forum, Future of Jobs Report 2023* - https://www.weforum.org/agenda/2023/05/future-of-jobs-2023-skills/

[145] Fabio Moioli in his LinkedIn post - https://www.linkedin.com/pulse/most-important-skill-future-ability-connect-dots-your-fabio-moioli/

[146] See for example *Creative Confidence: Unleashing the Creative Potential Within Us All* – Tom Kelly, David Kelly. Currency, Illustrated Edition (15 October 2013) and Thinking Fast and Slow. Daniel Kahneman, Penguin Press, 1st Edition (2 July 2012)
[147] Watch this video explanation https://www.youtube.com/watch?v=eg2pq4Mjeyo&t=153s
[148] http://cultureofempathy.com/references/Test.htm
[149] https://www.amazon.com/Empathy-Emotional-Intelligence-Harvard-Business/dp/1633693252/, also *I Hear You: The Surprisingly Simple Skill Behind Extraordinary Relationships*. Michael Sorensen Autumn Creek Press June 19,2017 and, specifically for lawyers https://scholarspace.manoa.hawaii.edu/server/api/core/bitstreams/ee91e472-2f23-4c2e-a219-b29e5349594a/content
[150] As explained in the first chapter of my first book
[151] *The Adaptation Advantage*, Heather McGowan and Chris Shipley, Wiley, March 27, 2020
[152] Ditto
[153] https://www.adaptationadvantage.com/

[154] See for example https://www.themakingbox.ca/aq-assessments, https://www.aqai.io/, and https://www.adaptability.org/.

[155] *The Adaptation Advantage,* Heather McGowan and Chris Shipley, Wiley, March 27, 2020
[156] https://www.adaptationadvantage.com/
[157] *World Economic Forum, Future of Jobs Report 2023* - https://www.weforum.org/agenda/2023/05/future-of-jobs-2023-skills/
[158] https://www.lawyerbrain.com/ research of lawyers in the U.S conducted by Dr Larry Richard
[159] Bonnano, 2005: Masten et all 1991
[160] WHO defines burnout here - https://www.who.int/news/item/28-05-2019-burn-out-an-occupational-phenomenon-international-classification-of-diseases
[161]See for example https://www.idrlabs.com/personal-resilience/test.php and https://www.totalbrain.com/mental-health-assessment/resilience-test/ and https://humanperformance.ie/resilience-test/
[162] Maslach Burnout Inventory https://www.healthlinkscertified.org/uploads/files/2022_11_16_19_56_57_Maslach-burnout-inventory-english.pdf
[163] See for example https://stressandresilience.com/burnout-resource-center/

and https://store.hbr.org/product/resilience-hbr-emotional-intelligence-series/10145 and https://www.google.com.au/books/edition/Building_Resilience_at_Work/Vw8NAaaaCR4C?hl=en&gbpv=1&dq=how+to+enhance+resilience+at+work&printsec=frontcover , *Building Resilience at Work*, Kathryn McEwen, Australian Academic Press, 2011, *The Resilient Lawyer- A Manual for Staying Well at Work*, Robyn Bradey 2014 - https://www.qls.com.au/getattachment/c198ec41-5b0b-4702-b236-625231d3b772/booklet-the-resilient-lawyer.pdf

[164] See for example https://ethics.org.au/, https://www.scu.edu/ethics/

[165] See for example https://www.aspenpublishing.com/Burk-Ethicallawyering, https://www.thehorizoninstitute.org/usr/library/documents/main/booklet-on-ethics-for-lawyers.pdf, https://www.olsc.nsw.gov.au/Documents/waling_ethical_tightrope_balancing_responsibilities_inhouse_counsel.pdf

[166] https://www.amazon.com/Human-Automation-Quest-Reclaim-Unique-ebook/dp/B099KQV3ZJ?tag=wwwfccom-20&asin=B099KQV3ZJ&revisionId=86dddd39&format=1&depth=1

[167] *Evaluating Mindset as a Means of Measuring Personal Innovativeness, Dennis A. Stauffer*. International Journal of Innovation Science Volume 7 · Number 4 · December 2015

[168] Other interesting mindsets to consider are the Positive Mindset mentioned by Dr Larry Richards. https://www.lawyerbrainblog.com/files/2021/09/Mindset-article-NALP-PDQ-September-2021-Dr-Larry-Richard.pdf I believe this is mostly covered as a component of the Growth Mindset. Also, the Learners Mindset, which I believe is also covered in the Growth Mindset and in what I refer to as a learning culture– see for example https://www.learnersmindset.com/lm-explained

[169] Carol Dweck is the author of *Mindset, The New Psychology of Success: How We Can Learn To Fulfil Our Potential.* Ballantine Books, 2016

[170] For example, https://www.simplypsychology.org/attitude-measurement.html and https://www.growthmindsetinstitute.org/growth-mindset/growth-mindset-for-business/mindset-assessment/

[171] *World Economic Forum The Future of Jobs Report 2018* at page 11

[172] Contributions do not necessarily have to be just coming up with creative ideas. There are many more ways that you can contribute to innovation.

[173] https://innovatormindset.com/take-im-2/ is an innovation mindset assessment tool.

[174] *Evaluating Mindset as a Means of Measuring Personal Innovativeness,* Dennis A. Stauffer. International Journal of Innovation Science Volume 7 ·

Number 4 · December 2015

[175] Depicted in Chapter 10 of my first book.

[176] See for example *Stolen Focus - Why you can't pay attention and how to think deeply again*. Johann Hari, Crown January 25, 2022 and *Make Time: How to Focus on What Matters Every Day*. Jake Knapp and John Zeratsky. Transworld Digital 27 September 2018

[177] Coined by Anders Ericsson, Florida State psychology professor and author of *Peak: Secrets from the New Science of Expertise*

[178] As explained in the discussion on leadership competency earlier in the book

[179] Except for business partnering and business leadership

[180] A reference to a quote mentioned in the first book from Carol Stubbings, when she was Global Leader People and Organisation at PWC when she said that you should *'think of yourself as a bundle of skills and capabilities and not a defined role or profession'*. See https://www.pwc.com/gx/en/services/people-organisation/workforce-of-the-future/workforce-of-the-future-the-competing-forces-shaping-2030-pwc.pdf

[181] See https://www2.deloitte.com/xe/en/insights/focus/human-capital-trends.html#navigating-the-end

[182] Peter Senge.

[183] *The Adaptation Advantage* referred to earlier.

Made in United States
Orlando, FL
04 November 2026

90200657R00174